UNF#CK YOUR FRIENDSHIPS

Using Science to Make and Maintain the Most Important Relationships of Your Life

FAITH HARPER, PhD, LPC-S, ACS, ACN

MICROCOSM PUBLISHING
Portland, Ore

UNFUCK YOUR FRIENDSHIPS
Using Science to Make and Maintain the Most Important Relationships of Your Life

© 2021 Faith G Harper, PhD, LPC-S, ACS, ACN
© This edition Microcosm Publishing 2021
First edition - 5,000 copies - September 23, 2021
ISBN 9781621060345
This is Microcosm #442
Edited by Elly Blue

To join the ranks of high-class stores that feature Microcosm titles, talk to your local rep: In the U.S. **COMO** (Atlantic), **FUJII** (Midwest), **BOOK TRAVELERS WEST** (Pacific), **TURNAROUND** (Europe), **UTP/MANDA** (Canada), **NEW SOUTH** (Australia/New Zealand), **GPS** in Asia, Africa, India, South America, and other countries, or **FAIRE** in the gift trade.

For a catalog, write or visit:
Microcosm Publishing
2752 N Williams Ave.
Portland, OR 97227
https://microcosm.pub/Friendships

Did you know that you can buy our books directly from us at sliding scale rates? Support a small, independent publisher and pay less than Amazon's price at **www.Microcosm.Pub**

Library of Congress Cataloging-in-Publication Data

Names: Harper, Faith G., author.
Title: Unfuck your friendships : using science to make and maintain the
  most important relationships of your life / Dr. Faith G. Harper.
Description: Portland, Ore. : Microcosm Publishing, [2021] | Includes
  bibliographical references. | Summary: "Friendship deserves more credit
  in a society obsessed with romantic and sexual relationships. In
  reality, friendship is the key to our mental and physical health,
  happiness, and social cohesion. Dr. Faith Harper, therapist and
  bestselling author of Unfuck Your Intimacy and Unfuck Your Boundaries
  applies brain science and her clinical and personal experience to help
  understand this vital type of relationship, offering insight into how to
  choose and make friends, sustaining and strengthening your friendships,
  friend group dynamics, friend breakups, setting excellent friendship
  boundaries, handling conflict, and managing all the different kinds of
  relationships we encounter in our lives. Includes a series of original
  advice columns honing in on the details that make our friendships
  work"-- Provided by publisher.
Identifiers: LCCN 2021033354 | ISBN 9781621063117 (trade paperback)
Subjects: LCSH: Friendship.
Classification: LCC BF575.F66 H38 2021 | DDC 177/.62--dc23
LC record available at https://lccn.loc.gov/2021033354

MICROCOSM · PUBLISHING

MICROCOSM PUBLISHING is Portland's most diversified publishing house and distributor with a focus on the colorful, authentic, and empowering. Our books and zines have put your power in your hands since 1996, equipping readers to make positive changes in their lives and in the world around them. Microcosm emphasizes skill-building, showing hidden histories, and fostering creativity through challenging conventional publishing wisdom with books and bookettes about DIY skills, food, bicycling, gender, self-care, and social justice. What was once a distro and record label was started by Joe Biel in his bedroom and has become among the oldest independent publishing houses in Portland, OR. We are a politically moderate, centrist publisher in a world that has inched to the right for the past 80 years.

Global labor conditions are bad, and our roots in industrial Cleveland in the 70s and 80s made us appreciate the need to treat workers right. Therefore, our books are MADE IN THE USA.

CONTENTS

INTRODUCTION

O f all the things that are incredibly important to our emotional and physical health, the one we don't talk about nearly enough is *friendship*.

We don't have control over our biological family and there isn't shit we can do about that. I mean, I did issue a formal complaint to the universe about it, but haven't gotten a response so far.

So until Alpha Centauri A gets back to me, we're gonna do the next best thing . . . choose the other people in our lives. The ones who nourish us, love us, see us for who we are, and encourage us to grow and achieve. And even though we can choose these people in ways that we can't choose to ignore our homophobic tia at family dinner, it isn't actually an easy task. Whether it be making friends, navigating the things that make friendships complicated, or just being a better friend, it's complex and weird and exhausting to go out and collect a group of humans to call your own.

When people ask me what kind of therapist I am, the short answer is "trauma therapist." It's kind of a record-scratch answer, but it is also the most accurate lens for all of the work that I do. It gets its octopus tentacles into so many aspects of our lives, including our friendships. No matter what brings a client in to see me, friend dynamics end up being part of the conversation at some point. And as a research nerd, I also know that we aren't just born with the tools to get it right. I want to give you those tools.

I'm going to talk about all the core stuff, like what friendship actually is, how to make friends, how to be a better friend, and friendship breakups. I'm gonna weigh in on the ancient question (ok, *couple decades old* question) of whether or not the internet is good for friendship. I'm also going to talk about more complex situations. The stuff that people are trying to unravel on the regular that more general information doesn't necessarily solve. I decided to tackle those advice-column style, since I got my start as a columnist in a no-longer-existent magazine and I miss it.

You'll also find that since friendships are, you know, another type of relationship, all this info will apply in some way to your family dynamics and romantic partnerships, even if it doesn't solve the problem of your homophobic tia directly.

Friendship isn't nearly the easy and intuitive process and concept that instagram makes it out to be. If so, we would all be so great at meeting people, collecting up the ones that we totally want to hang out with, and keeping them close for the rest of our lives. Eating cookies? Totally easy. Finding good friends and being a good friend? Definitely way harder. So let's talk about it.

WHAT IS FRIENDSHIP?

Okay, this may seem kind of dumb and obvious on the surface, but this is actually a really valid question. The easiest definition is: *an affectionate relationship based on a strong, voluntary interpersonal bond.* That is, someone who we are not stuck with by blood or legal means—which is to say, not our family[1]—that we pick out of the crowd and say "Ooooh, this one! I wanna go do shit with this weirdo!"

In his book *Friendship: Development, Ecology, and Evolution of a Relationship*, Daniel J. Hruschka points out that across time and cultures, friendships being *voluntary* connections between people is actually pretty unusual. Friendships have always been considered to be integral to our survival and happiness, so cultural rituals have always been created around the process. In some cultures, your parents picked your friends for you (big

---

1 Which isn't to say that you can't have a family member also be a friend, but choosing to expand a family relationship in that way is still a choice you make, right?

shudder) and big friendship ceremonies took place, similar to a wedding formalizing a romantic partner relationship.

Nowadays we have choice (thank fuck, double big shudder on the idea of my parents picking my friends) but there are still structures in place that tend to define/limit our friendship choices. Researchers have tried to formalize models of studying friendship and finally came up with one in the 1990s that we still use to this day. This model looks at two main categories of factors:

- Individual factors (our own personality traits, beliefs, values, approachability, social skills etc)

- Environmental factors (who is physically around us by nature of where we live, where we go, what we do).

Essentially, we are far more likely to become friend-persons with people who are pretty similar to us and are already in our regular environment. I met my best friend in grad school . . . he wasn't a fellow student, but close enough, he was actually my stats professor. We are both parents, political progressives, and have a super snarky sense of humor. The other people I would consider to be close friends are also people I have met through other friends, at places I've worked, or through organizations I volunteer with. And there is a super common theme of us all being snarky and incorrigible progressives who love books, tacos, and chisme.

But that still begs the question. If there are so many differences across cultures in how friendships are created and maintained, how can we even define the term effectively? My comment above about how friends are the people we pick out of a crowd and say "I wanna do shit with this weirdo!" may be a decent working definition for my culture, but not for everyone's. So how do we even "know" it's friendship? Dr. Hruschka found three themes in all types of friendships (arranged or created) that we can use to frame our understanding of what friending actually is:

- Positive (and mutual!) feelings of goodwill

- Unconditional assistance and aid when in need

- Gift-giving that is fun and frivolous rather than aid/need based. Like a baby yoda funko pop toy, not help with a car repair.

Dr. Hruschka was most interested in the idea of unconditional aid. It seems counterintuitive to evolutionary survival in many ways (more on that later when we discuss the barriers to making friends) but once someone is inside the bubble with us, it is a very steady construct. No matter past associations or the person's ability to provide future payback, it's something that we really do. If someone is our person, we love them. And we take care of them without tallying it as a zero-sum game.

Why We Need Friendships

We're wired for social connection. A connection to others, specifically others who *get* us, is a huge part of how we regulate our own emotional states and feel safe in the world. This is why you can be, say, admitted to the hospital and have a parade of doctors and nurses and techs and the like in and out of your room and still feel very, very alone and scared. No one is seeing and connecting to your emotional needs. When someone sees and accepts and loves our authentic self, we feel safer.

It also, interestingly enough, makes us bolder and braver. The idea that being attached to other people will make us codependent is utter bullshittery. The opposite is true. When we talk about "attachment issues" it is generally in relation to our relationships with the people who raised us and the people we end up with as our romantic partners. But (central theme of the book right here), attachment issues appear in any kind of interpersonal **relationships** we have. Relation means *a connection between*. And **attachment** is the nature of *how those connections are formed and maintained*. So all the flotsam and jetsam of our lives past and present (any old junk, tapes, mental health issues, trauma histories, etc) can affect these connections. Attachment is broken down into four types—secure, anxious, avoidant, and anxious-avoidant (disorganized) attachment.

I don't think anyone is shocked by the idea that our past family relationships and crappy exes have affected our current family relationships and romantic partnerships. But pointing out that this is also true of our friendships continues to be left out of the conversation. The best selling book on attachment theory is *Attached: The New Science of Adult Attachment and How It Can Help You Find and Keep Love* by Dr. Amir Levine, a psychiatrist and a neuroscientist. It's great and I recommend it regularly and have my office copy wander off almost as regularly. And it bums me out that it isn't marketed around the care and feeding of ALL of our relationships.

Because as Dr. Levine points out, being able to depend on someone doesn't just make us feel safer, it helps us believe in ourselves. We are more likely to go after our hopes and dreams because we know that someone is supporting us, hyping us, and cheering us along. And if need be, help catch us if we fall. And that is foundational to healthy friendships.

Friendships Are Relationships—Really Important Ones

Researchers have demonstrated that our psychological well being is tied first to romantic partners, then our friends, and lastly to our other family members. Friends are our #2 most important peoples and they move to #1 if we don't have a spouse or partner.

But friendships don't get the same level of respect (or even obsession) as sexual or romantic relationships in our culture.

The problem isn't so much that we intentionally decenter friendship but that we so heavily center couple-dom. Across culture, our mythology centers the romantic partnership . . . the idea that we are two halves of the same whole. Eve being created from Adam's rib. Or even darker if you're Plato. In Plato's *Symposium*, Aristophanes states that humans were originally four legged, four armed, and double sexed like some weird, land walking sea star. But Zeus felt threatened that humans may become as powerful as the Gods in this manner so sliced them in half, and now our heads face "toward the wound" so we are always seeking the other half of our "complete selves."

Ok, no pressure there.

Philosopher Elizabeth Brake created the word *amatonormativity*, a play on the word heteronormativity, using the Latin word *amatus* which means beloved. In her book *Minimizing Marriage: Marriage, Morality, and the Law*, she notes that the word refers to "the assumptions that a central, exclusive, amorous relationship is normal for humans, in that it is a universally shared goal, and that such a relationship is normative, in that it should be aimed at in preference to other relationship types." Take the fact that the fiction book market is 30% romance novels. Seriously, ⅓ of *all* fiction books are about sexitimes, and every other possible topic has to shove into the other 2/3rds.

Whether we are dead-ass single, in a relationship, or in some sort of situationship, we generally find our lives meaningful and fulfilling. Being boo'd up is not the litmus test for life happiness that the larger culture tries to impose upon us. Having good people in our lives in any way, shape, or form is. And the relationships we choose for ourselves, not the ones we are born into, or the ones that do not involve a level of romantic partnership, are a huge part of that.

Unless we *don't* have these good people in our lives.

How Loneliness Fucks Us Up

What happens when we don't have meaningful and fulfilling relationships? Our bodies start to release a slow drip of loneliness into our systems.

Loneliness is a feeling of dis-ease, discomfort, and sadness around perceived social isolation. Meaning, a feeling that our social needs are not being met in terms of quantity and, more importantly, quality.

Perceived is important. You can be surrounded by people, but not experience a sense of connection to any of them. Whether in the hospital with nurses and doctors poking at you constantly . . . or in the middle of a party that is supposed to be fun but the only person you are talking to is the cat hanging out in the corner.

You can also be pretty isolated and not consider yourself lonely. Plenty of people are perfectly content to live in the woods, all cottagecore as fuck, befriending the woodland creatures and hanging out quite rarely with other humans. Alone isn't lonely. Living alone isn't as strongly correlated to feeling alone as one may think. There are multiple benefits to solitude, including creativity, productivity, and self-awareness.

While people who are married or live with their families report less loneliness overall, people who feel alienated, unwanted, and unhappy in those situations often feel excruciatingly lonely compared to their neighbors who don't share a home with anyone.

We think of loneliness as being the most common among older adults. And while those numbers are high, it's even higher for younger people. Research demonstrates that self-reports of loneliness are 40% for individuals over the age of 65 but 80%

for individuals under 18. Those of us in the middle are the least likely to report loneliness, but it's still really prevalent.

So what is associated with increases in loneliness other than age? Immigrants in the US are far more likely to experience loneliness than US born individuals from the same ethnic group. And, unsurprisingly, members of the LGBT community also report more loneliness related to discrimation, stigma, and barriers to community and care. We can also experience loneliness epidemics. An economic dip in Japan in the aughts led to many men being out of work. So many in fact, some half a million people live as *hikikomori,* individuals withdrawn from social contact who don't leave their homes for months and even years at a time. Another big and obvious one is something like, oh you know, a pandemic and shut-down of our regular lives creating isolation, disconnection, and loneliness.

This is *state* loneliness. Meaning that something outside of ourselves is going on (we lose our job, we are working from home due to a pandemic, we are a queer punk in a conservative small town, etc) that limits our ability to interact with others both in general and in a meaningful authentic way.

But we have to discuss another aspect of loneliness you may not know about. And that's *trait* loneliness. While a state of being is a temporary experience, a trait is a more stable and consistent human characteristic. It turns out that all the external stuff that isolates us from quality connections only accounts for 52% of our loneliness. And trait loneliness makes up the other 48% in its entirety.

Researchers have been studying the underlying mechanisms of loneliness. What lights up in the brain when an experience of loneliness is reported by people? Turns out it is the nucleus accumbens (specifically in the ventral striatum), which is the region of the brain that is responsible for our reward processing. Meaning, that it is likely that trait loneliness is a dysfunction of social reward processing. Meaning, our brains don't recognize the connection to and with other people for shit sometimes.

And it looks like this big chunk of loneliness is genetic.

Or, more accurately, epigenetic.

Genetic means the heredity of certain genes. Like for the color of our eyes, our curly hair, cystic fibrosis, or sickle cell anemia. Epigenetics is the modification of our gene expression instead of our genetic code itself. Certain genes turn off and on based on our circumstances, and those gene expressions can also be passed along to future generations (at least up to *fourteen* generations, in case you are wondering). We inherit resilience. And we inherit trauma.

So, first off? I'm sorry.

I totally am very, very sorry.

I super-swear, pinky-promise that I wasn't trying to write about trauma in this book.

A book about friendship? That's a book about a lot of different aspects of emotional wellness. And maybe some stuff about how trauma can make it difficult to trust and make friends. But I had no idea that loneliness itself has deep roots in epigenetic trauma. At this point, my publisher probably thinks I'm just making shit up.

But here we are again at trauma. Trauma is an injury to our nervous system that occurs when something overwhelms our ability to cope. And in this instance, our ability to form and maintain secure attachments. It affects our ability to process social rewards, which then in turn creates a measure of dispositional set-point around loneliness. Just like some people are dispositionally happier than others? We all have a dispositional level of loneliness to contend with.

Whether a lack of care we experienced, or a lack of care that our ancestors experienced, that can translate to a sense of loneliness that has far less to do with our surroundings that most people realize. It's why some people are entirely happy living out in the woods with squirrel friends and others would feel that as a keening pain.

But none of this means that you have an unbudgeable loneliness set-point and no matter what you do you will always feel disconnected in the world. It means you may be *dispositionally lonely*, just like you may be dispositionally grumpy or dispositionally creative. It doesn't mean you're doomed forever and it isn't a life sentence of misery. It's something to be aware of in yourself.

And? It means doing some work around any trauma and attachment issues that get in the way of having the friendships you want so you can communicate more effectively and perceive relationship security when it's there and when it's not.

While the experience of loneliness varies wildly in different people, it still serves as a primal reminder and whatever level it exists. Loneliness is as cellular as hunger, telling us we need the nourishment of connection, just like physical hunger tells us we need food. And it is not about just needing support, because we can totally get that from a therapist. It's about the mutuality of that support. We are fed as much by doing things for others as having people do things for us.

Loneliness is Bad for Our Health

If you read my book *Unfuck Your Body,* you got a minicourse on how emotional issues affect the physical body, and loneliness is no different. The expression of our genes (epigenetics) gets altered by the trauma of loneliness, causing inflammation and early cell death. It's as bad for us as literal poison.

The impact of loneliness on our physical health is akin to smoking 15 cigarettes a day. That was a huge headline a few years ago, even before the COVID-19 pandemic rolled up its sleeves and said *"I'll show you lonely, motherfuckers."*

As clickbaity as the headline was, it's also accurate, as demonstrated by researchers over and over in recent decades. The impact on our mental health and physical health are equally frightening. So much so that former U.S. Surgeon General Vivek Murthy ended up declaring loneliness as the health issue he most wanted to tackle.

Social isolation increases our risk of heart disease, stroke, dementia, depression, anxiety, psychosis, personality disorders, low self worth, and suicide. Meaning people who didn't already have these health issues and reported loneliness were far more likely to end up having them when researchers followed up with them later. And for people who did already have these health issues, the people who were also lonely were far more likely to have hospital visits, complications, and even die due to their disease. Loneliness accelerates illness.

Of course this is looking at existing data over time, this isn't a controlled experiment. Researchers got our backs on that, too. One study used hypnotherapy to induce feelings of social connectedness. The negative way the study participants viewed themselves so immediately suggests that our connections provide a literal support for our sense of self that quickly falls apart when those supports are removed. And that changes our emotional well-being and then starts to attack our physical body.

And crappy friendships do the same thing. Bert Uchino, a social psychologist, has studied not just the existence of friendship but also how good they actually are. And related that data to physical health issues. What he terms *aversive* relationships means wholly shitty. Whether a toxic partnership, a batshit family, or a really awful "friend." And these aversive relationships are clearly linked to the same negative physical and emotional health outcomes

Questions to consider

- How would you differentiate being alone and being lonely?

- How do each of these present in your own life?

- What kinds of circumstances have made loneliness more awful for you?

- What kind of impact has loneliness had on you?

What Makes a Friendship Healthy

So if loneliness is awful, and crappy friendships are as awful for us as no friendships, how do we have healthy ones? Is a good friendship like what Supreme Court Justice Potter Stewart said about porn ("I know it what I see it") or is it something we can deconstruct in such a way that we have a more solid understanding of what we are looking for? I mean, obviously the latter or we wouldn't have much of a book, right?

I've written about relational-cultural theory enough times at this point that if you read my books on the regular you have already seen me whip out this particular soapbox. RCT came about in

the 1970s from women theorists and clinicians who were really tired of the traditional psychological model that insisted that you should work toward self-reliance rather than interdependence. Many decades in, we have the research to demonstrate that yes, these theorists were correct when saying that we need connection just like we need food and water.[2]

We grow in and toward connection and suffer in isolation. Our bodies are designed to manage stress and trauma and pain by the presence of someone who knows us and loves us. That connection literally changes our brains, and offers protection

---

2 Another core tenet of RCT is that our mental health is deeply impacted by society. That's the "culture" part. Meaning racism, sexism, heterosexism, ableism, etc are all instrumental in causing mental health issues.

in the very worst of times. Interdependence, not independence, is how we survive, but until the middle of the 20th century, that was considered foundational to mental health. One of the founders of relational-cultural therapy was Jean Baker Miller. And a model she created that we still use today are the elements of a growth-fostering relationship which she termed *the five good things in practice.*

If making friends is so important but so difficult? And if we have limited time and energy and even brain capacity to balance all of our relationships well? How do we "grade" our friendships? And it came to me, maybe because I am an RCT trained therapist so that's the first place I go all the time, that Dr. Miller's recipe for a growth-fostering relationship is a simple and elegant solution. So let's look at what they are.

1. **Each person feels a greater sense of "zest."** A good relationship makes us feel energized. Even if you are an introvert who always needs a recharge period after being around people, your best people nourish more than they take. These are the relationships that bring out our aliveness.

2. **Each person feels more able to act—and does act.** A good relationship acts as a secure base that allows us to be braver than we would

on our own. Our best friends are also our wingpeople and the people most likely to hype what they see in us that we may struggle to see in ourselves.

3. **Each person has a more accurate picture of themself and the other person(s).** A growth-fostering relationship makes us both compassionate and open to betterment. We see ourselves as deserving of love and capable of loving and also able to continue to mature and grow as human beings.

4. **Each person feels a greater sense of worth.** I don't know anyone who hasn't struggled to recognize their inherent value as a human being. This is likely a product of our current culture, but growth-fostering relationships help reflect that value back to us, making it easier for us to believe in our own value.

5. **Each person feels more connected to the other person(s) and feels a greater motivation for connections with other people beyond those in the specific relationship.** Good relationships lead to more good relationships. Once we learn that there are people in the

world that are worth our time and effort, we start to seek them out and trust ourselves to find and cherish the ones that deserve it.

Okay, awesome. But how do we get there? Or at least, how can we tell if we are heading in that direction? In *Attached,* Amir Levine created an acronym of points to remember when judging if a relationship is a secure one (yes, we fucking love our acronyms . . . and it's probably because therapist types can't remember stuff, not because we think our clients can't). Dr. Levine uses CARRP, while still cautioning people that not one size fits all. Meaning all relationships are different, so perfection in all categories is not the goal. However, this is a way to figure out what the strengths and limitations of each relationship is. And if you end up with a fully operational CARRP, hold on to them because they're a badass friend.

Consistency. Are they in and out of your life without any logical reason? Not like, they disappear during finals cuz they are a student or tax season cuz they're an accountant. But do they show up for your weekly hiking date (or cancel properly if they can't make it)? Do they check in with you as much as you check in with them? Or are they the type of person who disappears the minute they have something "better" to do but when they are bored they hit you up to go hang out.

Availability. Availability ties into consistency, but is also about what you expect from a friendship. Someone may not be blowing you off but are genuinely busy, or are an exhausted introvert who wants to go crawl under the covers rather than attend a cooking class. And that's all super reasonable, but they may not be your cooking class friend. Availability is also a chips-down question. I'm a pretty busy human on the regular and can't hang at a whim, but if the shit hits the fan with a friend of mine I clear my schedule and show the fuck up.

Reliability. Reliability is also part of the chips-down question. Can you count on them if you need something? My friend Patti is that person. I may not see her or talk to her for long periods of time (we are both busy as fuck) but if I texted her today and said *"on September 19th can you meet me in Dallas and bring 37 folding chairs, a lifeguard's whistle, and a monkey?"* she will three-thousand-percent be there, and would probably pick me up a coffee on the way. Dr. Levine suggests testing new people in this regard with a low-risk ask so you are aware of what their limits of reliability are. You want to ask someone if they can bring ice to the party, before you expect them to steal a monkey and drive it to Dallas for you, right? If they handle the ice then they might be your go-to if you need to be bailed out of jail.

Responsiveness. Responsiveness is a big one that puts the first three into perspective. If they respond consistently, and/or when important that is a huge indicator of a good friend. My best friend and I may not respond to every dumb meme we send each other, but if it's important? And we tell each other it's important? Absolutely. When you are sharing details of your life, do your friends demonstrate that they are hearing, not just listening? Do they pay attention to your expressed needs and not just their own?

Predictability. Being able to judge our level of friendship with someone is far easier when we have a general idea of how they will act and react in certain situations, which often ties into the above. Do they show the fuck up when they say they will? Are they kind and supportive without letting you get away with sitting on your pity potty for weeks on end? That's your people.

So many of us go through life thinking our friend-picker, nevermind our partner-picker, is broken. If there was an easy equation we'd all be using it, and of course there isn't. Even for CARRP, or for the *5 Good Things* for that matter, there is no magical rating scale. But it is a good framework for considering the investment you want to make in a relationship. Whether you have a tendency to jump in and then get taken advantage of, or you've had such a wrecked history with people that you don't trust anyone, having some kind of method for figuring out if someone is worth investing in and how much.

Types of Friendship

Is any particular breakdown on friendship types the "best" one? Nope. And do we need to identify types of friendships at all? Not to keep the planet spinning, no. But it can be helpful to recognize that there are many kinds of friendships and all of them play an important role in us being happy, healthy, connected, non-lonely beings. And it's *also* helpful to recognize that we may be asking the wrong person for the level of support we are needing. Or to recognize that we want some deeper connections than the ones we have at the moment.

Friendship isn't something that has been written about extensively. Romance gets the top award for all the pontificating philosophers, except for Aristotle. Aristotle was a big fan of friendships at every point of a person's life. The study of friendship involves trying to tease out the types of friendships that exist in people's lives and it turns out that Aristotle's three categories of friends work well. He stated that we have:

1. Friendships of **Utility**

2. Friendships of **Pleasure**

3. Friendships of **Virtue**

And while I'm going to use more modern ideas and terms about friendships in this chapter, all of them do fit nicely into Aristotle's original categories.

Friendships of utility are the friendships that have developed as a functional tool of mutual benefit. Think of the coworker that has your back, that you cover for each other with the boss, knock out tasks quickly because you work well together, while cracking jokes, listening to the same music, and agreeing on where to get lunch. But they probably aren't the one you call to process your fight with your sibling.

Friendships of pleasure are the friendships that are based on sharing an interest. This may be your buddies from your tabletop gaming group or your running club. Y'all hang because you both have the same hobby or interest that you can engage in together. But again these aren't the first people you call when the shit hits the fan, even though they might join in to help you out when you break your leg.

And friendships of virtue is the term that Aristotle used to describe the deep and meaningful appreciation of someone. These are the people with whom we meet all of Dr. Hruschka's requirements for a close relationship. However the relationship started, maybe as a friendship of utility or pleasure, we have chosen to continue to invest in that relationship as it deepens into something more complex and long-lasting.

These categorizations are pretty tightly contained and of course there is a lot of space in between. There is no way to categorize all the different nuances, like the "person I've been hanging out with more and can talk to about kid stuff but not really about partner stuff I don't think."

I don't mean (and I don't think Aristotle meant) for these categories to represent the be-all end-all way of defining our chosen, platonic relationships. Life is more wibbily-wobbily than that, and includes the "friend from school that I've been hanging out with more and I can def talk to them about kid stuff, but maybe not partner stuff yet." But it is helpful to think about this relational continuum as we are thinking about best supporting healthy relationships in our lives.

Acquaintance-People

What Aristotle called friends of utility or pleasure, we tend to call acquaintances, and what researchers call *weak ties*. Not a great word, but it is the one coined by Stanford sociologist Mark Granovetter in 1973 as a catch-all for the other people in our orbit that comprise the other people with which we have some familiarity. He meant it as the counterbalance to our strong tie friendships, Aristotle's friendships of virtue. Our acquaintance friends such as the person we work out with at the gym a few times a week (friendships of pleasure) or the barista that knows our order and asks about our cat every time we see them (friendships of utility).

These acquaintanceships are also incredibly important to combating loneliness. We may not even know the barista's name but we know they also have a cat and they are going back to school to study engineering this Fall. Chatting for a couple of minutes is a nice part of both of your days. Engaging with people in this manner helps us feel in-and-of our community. There may not be a huge amount of depth to our interactions but it widens our circle of connection and helps us feel seen. It also expands our exposure to different ideas and ways of being.

This is the category that took the hardest hit because of Covid-19. We may not have been able to spend time with our close friends because of isolation, but we remained in some level of contact. But we lost our connections with "funny corner store dude" and "nice lady who works out at the gym at the same time as I do" and those lost connections have taken a mental health toll, not just in terms of the loss of connection but the loss of exposure to difference. When much of our pandemic connectivity moved online, it also moved into echo chambers. Meaning, we sought out people more like us rather than naturally running into people that are somewhat different from us. And yes, some social scientists attribute the rise in groups like Q-Anon to this level of echo-chamber connection.

Chosen Family

Aristotle's friendship-of-virtue is probably best related to the modern idea of chosen family. The SAGE Encyclopedia of Marriage, Family, and Couples Counseling says, *"chosen families are nonbiological kinship bonds, whether legally recognized or not, deliberately chosen for the purpose of mutual support and love."* Chosen family is the result of us cultivating friendships that enrich our lives outside of our biological families, or help us fill in the gaps left by our biological families. Examples of this being done in a formal way can be seen in ballroom culture in New York in the 80s and 90s (honored beautifully in the FX series Pose, which was based on the documentary Paris is Burning). And from this embracing of the idea of chosen family, came a new idea in the past decade.

The term *queerplatonic*[3] applies to the deep and meaningful relationships that we form outside of biological family units and

3 Quasiplatonic is another common term. Quirkyplatonic is less known but also appears in the literature.

romantic/sexual partnerships. The platonic part we get, but why queer? Kaz and S. E. Smith coined the term in 2010 to reference "difference" rather than limiting the relationship to having a non-cis or non-hetero component to it. It's different because it has a depth beyond our societal rules around friendship. There is a partnership aspect of the relationship that makes our typical words about friendship fail.

Because language is culturally shaped, and this case by the aforementioned amatonormativity, there has historically been no good word for describing this person in your life, the term *zucchini* became popular, also coined by Kaz and Smith. It started as a joke but became canon because the silliness of it matches the silliness that our current vernacular is so ill-suited to describe the depth of these relationships. Which also exists as more evidence of the amatonormativity Elizabeth Blake wrote about.

And our zucchinis, should we be lucky enough to have them, are life-saving relationships. They are essentially our family of choice that are built outside the traditional ideal of biological connection and connection through marriage. Even if we have great partners and bio families, our queerplatonic relationships, our chosen family, our friendships of virtue, are equally sustaining and important. And I'd argue maybe more so because we build them to be exactly what we need. If these relationships don't exist in the cultural rule book, then we don't have to consider any of those rules in their formation.

Questions to consider

- What people in your life do you enjoy your regular contact with on the acquaintance level?

- What do you enjoy about these interactions?

- What benefits do you get from them?

- Who do you consider your closest friends? Do you think of them as chosen family?

- How has having close friends provided you a different level of support (whether or not your bio family is great or awful or just in-between)?

Making Friends

Some of you already have really great friends and are reading this just to hone your friend-person skill set (go you). The rest of you may be reading this because you have noticed that you don't have the kind of friendships that you really would like to have. But no matter your situation, life is all twisty-turny, and tuning up our friend-making skills is never a waste of time. We are all continuously learning and growing and making new friends along the way.

If having friends is so fucking important to our wellbeing it should be something pretty easy to do and something we would be reasonably skilled at doing. But alas, neither are really true. There are tons of perfectly competent fully functional human beings (I'm including all of us in that category) that struggle to make friends. It's actually pretty difficult. While there are evolutionary reasons we need friends, there are also evolutionary reasons that they are really difficult to form. And that difficulty is part of what makes them so valuable to us. And that actually makes sense, friendships are important to us and incredibly valuable *because* they can be so difficult to form.

We Have a Limited Amount of Physical Time and Mental Energy

Raise your hand if you are a competent human being in many areas but still find it weirdly difficult to make friends. Now look around at how many other people have their hands up along with us. This is super common and not near an indication of your unfriendability. An article in *OZY Presents the Sunday Magazine* from 4/11/2021 asked readers whether they found making friends hard. Nearly half said yes, and that it has gotten increasingly difficult as they have gotten older. Readers were totally self-aware in their reports that their time feels more valuable, they've gotten fussier about what is important to them, they are less interested in trying new things where they might forge new connections, and they've started to not trust people as much.

And what if you move a lot? Or even once? Another study commissioned by the people who run Patook (an app designed for making platonic friends) found that we don't feel comfortable with making friends in a new place for about 5 years. That's a big chunk of time somewhere feeling really fucking isolated.

Why is making friends so hard and why does it take so long? John Cacioppo, a social neuroscientist who spent his career studying loneliness, found that we have a built-in evolutionary bias to proceed on the side of caution. In an interview he did with The Atlantic in 2017, he stated:

> *"If I make an error and detect a person as a foe who turns out to be a friend, that's okay, I don't make the friend as fast, but I survive. But if I mistakenly detect someone as a friend when they're a foe, that can cost me my life. Over evolution, we've been shaped to have this bias."*

So it would make sense that in a new place we would be even more on guard. And that as we gain years on the planet, it's easier to hit social oversaturation. In the 1990s, anthropologist Robin Dunbar posited that we have a cognitive limit to the number of people with which we can maintain a social relationship over time, based on correlating primate brain size with the size of each primates average social group. He found that for humans that number is about 150. So our work team, our gym buddies, and our zucchinis all add to this number, and we can easily become oversaturated and overwhelmed.

In order to bridge the gap between evolutionary and social psychology (we need friends for survival and it's also difficult to meet and trust new people). Enter *Communicate Bond Belong (CBB) Theory* to help make both of these truths make sense.

CBB theory posits that all social interactions require an expenditure of energy (fucking got that right), but not all of them are designed to fill that need for connection.

We have this constant math equation going on trying to balance investing and conserving our (social) energy and adapting to different environments and obligations. So friendship seeking is actually designed to be a pretty strategic thing we do, not an intuitive one. We are always considering if we should invest hours in a new friendship versus strengthening current ones and what are the potential safety concerns for us in any of these exchanges.

In short? We're busy. And overwhelmed. And not just in a "hahahaha, that's life tho!" kind of way but in a very real *neurological* kind of way. So making that process more conscious can be incredibly helpful to our goals around having quality friendships.

And, Let's Be Real, We Tend to Feel Like Crap About Ourselves

Of course, the overwhelm isn't the entirety of it. Our own self-worth is also a pretty exhausting hobgoblin to live with. In all the research on combating loneliness, a huge portion of the interventions found to be useful are about dealing with our own wonky wiring. That is, helping us read others more accurately. The most useful treatment for people who struggle to make friends is treating their *maladaptive social cognition*. That is, their low self-worth. We tend to think that people hate us (or at least don't like us) and don't want us around.

And even if our self-worth is fine, another big issue, especially for my neurodiverse people, is missing cues. Some of us don't catch when we accidentally did say or do something that upset someone else, and we're going blithely along our way, thinking everything is fine. You know, social skills. That nebulous and broad category that defines all the spoken and unspoken rules about navigating communications and interactions with others. Something that you don't have to be neurodiverse to struggle with.

Good news though. Skills are learned abilities, not innate ones. Social skills don't spring fully formed from a natural aptitude at peopleing. People constantly tell me how good I appear at connecting with others, and the truth is all my social skills were learned clunkily and were very hard won. And my inner self is still a deeply awkward 11 year old.

If the issue is primarily your own sense of worth, this is where therapy can be useful. There may be some trauma to unpack, especially related to how you were raised and how that is affecting your present. Doing some self-propelled work around your attachment style (chances are it's not secure attachment, right?) can also be helpful.

If it is mostly a matter of social skills, that is likely more the domain of an occupational therapist, a skills trainer, or a coach. Especially if you're neurodiverse. It can also be super helpful to check out books or videos about nonverbal communication like facial expressions and body language. Joe Navarro is a former FBI agent who is a specialist in non-verbal body language. His interest in the field started when he immigrated to the US from Cuba and was plopped in an American school without speaking the language. All of his early communication was nonverbal, which led to his career. His book *What Every Body Is Saying* is super useful, even if you are already pretty decent at reading body language, and maybe lifesaving if you struggle with it.

Other social skills tools that can be helpful include initiating and maintaining conversations in ways that are setting appropriate, connecting to empathy, and asserting boundaries.

Finding Friends

So we know making friends is hard but it's not impossible. How do we actually do it?

First let me nod back to the two main categories of factors I mentioned early in the book. We have our individual factors (our own personality traits, beliefs, values, approachability, social skills etc) and our environmental factors (who is physically around us by nature of where we live, where we go, what we do). Taking on an objective like Operation: Excellent Friends means pushing out of the comfort zone of both. Ugh, I know. Gross. But! We are gonna *ease* our way into it to make it slightly less terrifying. And I just made an epic dad joke, please forgive me.

EASE Your Way into New Friendships

But how do you actually go about making those friends? Back to Dr. Cacioppo and his research on loneliness again. He created an acronym around building social connections. And he intentionally made the acronym EASE because it's something we legit have to ease ourselves into if we have been living feral for a while.

E means extend yourself. But safely and in manageable increments. You don't have to Leeroy Jenkins yourself into stuff, you are allowed to try just a little bit of something outside of your comfort zone. Think taking a two hour cooking class rather than signing up for a semester-long event. Or you can try a drop-in tai chi class before signing up for a 20 class package.

Some other types of ways to extend yourself might include saying yes to invitations more often (with an escape plan . . . don't panic!), makin casual and open invitations (like announcing at work "Hey, I'm walking down to the corner store for a soda, anyone wanna walk with me?"), biking a different route and . . . you know . . . like smiling and waving at people, hanging out at a new coffee shop, complimenting someone on their cool t-shirt, asking them about the boots they are wearing and you've considered buying, engaging thoughtfully with someone's social media posts, or really anything that gets you out of your daily routines.

A means have an action plan. There are two parts to this. One is doing the mental work around recognizing that not everyone is going to want to be your friend. And that someone being disinclined to hang out with your *is a rejection of your offer, not a rejection of your personhood.* And also to have an action plan around making new connections. Having some scripts in your back pocket about how to open a conversation up and keep one going. That kind of thing. If extending yourself is a small trial run with limited investment in time and other resources, it keeps you from needing to do all the mentally fatiguing work around a complex action plan, right?

S means seek collectives. Look for groups of people who like the same shit you like where they do it together. This is always my biggest piece of advice to anyone looking at expanding their social network for any reason (friending, dating, relationshipping). Because our time is limited and precious, we should expand in directions of things we like. Or things we are interested in that we always wanted to explore and see if we like. If you are interested in making sushi and take a sushi-making class, you may meet some cool people. But even if you don't, you still did something interesting with your time. And if you spend it volunteering for something that is important to you? Then you get the bonus humaning level-up of having put good into the world. Other places to expand your social network might include going to shows or open-mic nights, attending spiritual or religious gatherings that vibe with your own belief system, You don't have to join a running group if you don't run unless someone is chasing you. There are meet-ups for going to movies together, too!

And the final E means expect the best. Meaning go in with a good attitude. This doesn't mean you walk in determined to meet your new bestie, but you are going in with an open mind to the experience . . . and your face will reflect that. You will be far more approachable without your fight face on. And it provides a helpful mental counterbalance to that evolutionary hyper-vigilance to social threat. You know how some people just vibe as safe and friendly? Something about them creates that sense that they're good people. How can you create that same sense of openness and acceptance in yourself?

Ok, hot stuff . . . now go put something on your calendar!

Questions to consider

- What factors have most gotten in the way of you expanding and deepening your friendship circle?

- What would be the easiest "tweak" you could incorporate to expand your friend-making opportunities?

Making Friends Online

Now that we carry tiny internet machines in our pockets at all times (that theoretically make phone calls?) there has been growing interest in the idea of *omgponies technology is ruining everything.* Nowadays there's a lot of concern that we use social media and online communities in ways that isolate us and make us more lonely and isolated and less empathetic—and that these "fake" online friendships ruin us for "real" friendship. Okay, boomer.

Pearl-clutching over technology has been a constant human complaint, even before we had the pearls to clutch. Socrates was furious with the idea of written language, stating that it would be terrible for our memories, because if things were written down we would know we could just access it later and didn't need to remember it now.

Which, yeah. Literally was the point.

So new technology tends to create a lot of *hot water burns baby* fear in us. Anything new does. And being careful of how something new may affect us in both positive and negative ways is smart. So now that we have more than a decade of smart phone data available to crunch data on it turns out being online so much isn't really causing any damage to our ability to connect with each other. Nor is it the best thing ever. It's just another way of being human.

But like with anything else, how we use this increased connectivity is what matters.

Essentially, the best way to be online is to use it as a waystation. Meaning connecting through social media so you can build from there and connect with people one-on-one, and hopefully in person. Like joining a local hiking group on Facebook then actually meeting everyone for a weekend hike. Or joining a local zoom support group and exchanging numbers with someone else in the group who you really want to spend more time with. If you are a queer punk in Podunk, Arkansas, meeting others face to face may not be possible, but having individual and authentic online connections with others who share your experience absolutely still counts. If it's y'all's own Discord channel because you are all flung around the planet so be it. When used in that way, research shows that being online is associated with less loneliness.

But when social media (and the internet in general) is a destination instead of a stop along the way, that's when we feel lonelier than before. Friendship is about being seen and accepted by others, so interacting online in a non-authentic ways . . . no matter how many thirst-trap likes you receive on instagram . . . makes us feel like shit. Fake representation of ourselves can give us a little ego boost, but does not lead to connection. And if we catch ourselves scrolling endlessly or checking our inbox when we are at an event with other people (especially people we like) then there might be a problem.

And this is where I dust off my other old-lady advice is to think about what you share and with whom. Putting your vulnerability out there is difficult enough in face-to-face interactions, but once you go online then you have the added issue of screen-shot proof. Or, if you are fairly public with your social media, later issues with schools and employers. I have so many clients, especially the younger ones, tell me that finding their people online has been lifesaving mental health support. And I absolutely agree with them. But also keep in mind that just because you are *trusting,* doesn't mean that someone is *trustworthy.* A written-record presence makes the stakes higher, and you deserve safe relationships no matter how they are formed.

Questions to consider

- In what ways do you use social media that promotes finding and deepening friendships?

- In what ways has social media gotten in the way of finding and deepening friendships?

- What's your action plan for ensuring that social media becomes a positive tool instead of one that leads to doomscrolling in sadness and despair?

Lessons from Our TV Friends

A fascinating human-brain thing we do is connect to individuals we see in the media and our brains code them as "friends." This happens on all kinds of media. Musicians, authors, social media content creators, etc. Even fictional characters—they don't have to be an actual person for us to create a connection. Psychologists have started using the term *parasocial interaction* (PSI)[4] to describe the relationship our brains experience when connecting to a media personality while engaging in the medium through which you know them.

We're not talking about the person you don't know that well on Twitter but you follow each other and comment to each other

---

4   Term coined by researchers Donald Horton and Richard Wohl in 1956

and chat sometimes. This is talking about Richard Marx, who you follow on Twitter, who is hilarious and political and engages with his followers. Over time, a series of parasocial interactions becomes a *parasocial relationship* over time. Probably especially so for people who seem the most unguarded and authentic. So your brain declares Richard (or whomever) one of your friends. While it isn't a reciprocal relationship in reality, and a good chunk of your brain knows that to be true, another part is absolutely smitten with this famous bestie.

While the idea of parasocial interactions isn't new, the science-y part of how they affect us hasn't really been studied until fairly recently. In 2009, researchers Jaye Derrick, Shira Gabriel, and Kurt Hugenberg developed the *Social Surrogacy Hypothesis*. They looked at multiple studies that found that these parasocial relationships serve to buffer us against loneliness and the assorted mental and physical health issues that can occur when we experience chronic loneliness.

Our ability to form this kind of relationship can be taken advantage of in good ways and nefarious ones. A rock star who encourages everyone to get an overdue cancer screening may get further than your MIL yelling about it. Author Shea Serrano (*The Rap Year Book* among others) helped raise six figures through social media for the food bank that serves Central Texas when COVID-19 pandemic layoffs were at their peak.

But there are also the celebs that use their influence to have you buy that diet tea that makes you shit your pants at work. And fuck them for making you feel like you need to diet and you need to buy something gross to do it. In short? Parasocial relationships tend to be bad for our body image and for aggressive behavior, though both happen when we have a predisposition to either starting out . . . watching John Wick isn't going to make you beat up people if that's not in your nature.

We also experience the mental health effect of parasocial breakups. The grief people experience when, for example, their favorite show ends is a very real thing. And probably explains how personally we take it when it doesn't end the way we wanted it to.

But there are also huge positives. As mentioned earlier, when we are lonely and/or isolated, we get a sense of belonging that our brains really need. And these relationships are good for our learning in general. An actor discussing apartheid on their insta live may be our first exposure to something really important (and something we likely didn't hear about in school). And these relationships are a healthy part of our identity formation in general. It helps us see ways of being in the world and possibilities for our own lives. When someone you grew up watching comes out, that may help you recognize that you can also come out and have a happy and healthy life

So I'm not telling you to disengage from these connections. They are powerful and overall quite positive. And quite likely have saved lives over the years—especially during times of enforced isolation, like COVID. But if you are in a situation where most of your connections are parasocial and you would like to build connections that are more bidirectional, these relationships can provide some really good clues on how friendships nourish you.

Questions to consider

- What is it that you most admire about this individual/character? How are they aspirational?

- What do you most connect to with this individual/character? How are they relatable?

- What does that tell you about the qualities you are looking for when inviting people into your life?

Unfuck Your Friendships

If you've read this far I have hopefully convinced you of why friendships are worth investing in, what are the ingredients of a good friendship, and how to take on the super-awkward task of making new friends. And now *this* part of the book is about making sure your current (and future) friendships get properly fed and watered so they stay healthy and awesome.

I think we can conceptualize why friendships fail by understanding what makes them so stressful to begin with. Letty Cottin Pogrebin, in her 1987 book *Among Friends*, notes that there are four epic contradictions in how we experience our friendships.

1) **The Stress Factor.** In ye olden days of yore, friendships were stress relievers. No pressure, the fun part of our lives. But now they can be stress producers, something else we have to

manage along with all the other shit in our lives.

2) **Lack of Consensus.** We all use the word friendship but all have totally different ideas of what friendship means. For example, you might say "my friend" and mean someone who is part of your RPG group and you think is cool and enjoy hanging out with, but they might hear you say that and feel awkwardly obligated to make you a bridesmaid in their wedding. Different *meanings* equal different *expectations* equal *epic fails*.

3) **The Critical Stance.** We expect more from friends than from family. This seems backwards, but it makes sense. Family is chosen for us, friends are something we choose. But you know how we choose our friends? Based on the sense of loyalty and trust we feel from them. More than shared social status or any other friendship determination factor, we are attracted to people with *value systems* similar to our own. They reinforce and validate our beliefs about the world, and they make us feel safest in our interactions with them and with others. They have our backs, so to speak. So we

expect way more expert awesomeness from them, and get way more butthurt when they are human and fail to meet our expectations. Makes sense, right? You can't un-family Uncle Cyril for being a racist creeper, but you can definitely un-friend someone whose values don't align with your own.

4) **Self-Reliance vs. Connection.** Pogrebin's book predates the neuro research that shows we are hardwired to connect to others, but she nailed it when she said we have a deep seated desire for intimate connection with others but there is a traditional Western cultural message that we should be self-reliant and protect our privacy. How hard is it to show people who we really are, in all our awkwardness and uncoolness. Especially when we tend to convince ourselves that everyone is far more together than we are and we don't want to glom our hot-messness on them.

All of these things equate to serious pressure in the end. Friendships can end up carrying more weight than many of them can bear for a sustained amount of time. This can work for a short period of time, but long-term you have to work to relieve the pressure. Because friendship is hard work. And people change. And circumstances change. And the very mechanisms that create friendships are often what lead to their dissolution. Or at least to really awkward fights.

But never fear, I'm going to give you some tools from my secret therapist toolbox, and we're also going to talk about boundaries, communication, and all that good stuff that makes any kind of relationship work.

Attention and Attunement

Feeling a sense of connection and security with our friends and knowing that they're listening to us and that they really see us is a key ingredient in friendship. But I see how hard it is for so many people to demonstrate that they are connected and listening. Not because the internet broke us, but because it's not an innate skill, it's a learned one. Some people learn it through mimicry, if they grew up around people that were good at it. But if you had a pretty chaotic childhood, or if you are neurodiverse, you may really struggle with *attention and attunement*.

In order to interpret someone else's needs we have to be paying attention to them like it's our job. Attention over time teaches us about how people express themselves, allowing us to tune in at a deeper level when they are demonstrating that they need us to. Remember earlier when I said our friendships operate as a secure base? Meaning if we know people have our backs we are bolder and braver in our everyday lives? We have an inner knowing of who has our backs based on who is attuned to us. Attunement is *understanding*.

But just because these things are important doesn't make them come naturally to us. We use mirror neurons to monitor and interpret the behavior of other humans by feeling with them. Mirror neurons weren't discovered until 1991 and became one of those big leaps of understanding about how social cognition works. Neurodiverse individuals demonstrate neural interaction differences in their mirror neuron systems, as *do individuals with post traumatic stress disorder*. So when we have trouble showing you that we're listening to you, it isn't that we lack empathy, it's that we lack the ability to connect with it.

Attention and attunement makes us better partners, better parents, better co-workers, and better friends. And many people just don't know how to do that. So I think it's unfair when attachment theorists encourage people to look at others with full attention and expect our mirror neurons to kick in and do their thing (not naming names, but yes this is real advice from a very well known best-selling author, and not the one I mentioned earlier in this book).

If we don't do that well, we come up with adaptive strategies that often get us in trouble. A common one I see is when kind-hearted people activate their empathy by relating the story a friend is telling them to a similar experience of their own. The internal process may go something like: *Holy shit, their dad is sick? I remember when my dad had surgery 5 years ago. I was so worried, and such a mess for weeks. I bet that's how they feel and that's fucking awful. I'm really hurting for them right now.*

What gets these kind-hearted people in a confused state of trouble, however, is not their internal process, but that becoming their out-loud voice. And the friend is now thinking: *Wow, can I just have my experience right now rather than making it about yours?* I've seen over and over and over that someone working to relate with empathy is perceived as taking over the conversation to "make it about themself" when that was never their intent.

I think a couple of things should happen in these situations. If we know we have a tendency to be a relater-empathic (I just made that up, pass it on) we can work to keep that process internal so it doesn't look like we are centering our own experience. And if we know relater-empathics we can recognize that's what they're doing, it's not meant to be the least bit unkind, and grace always gets us further in life than butthurt.

But that aside? We can also learn a new way of connecting to our empathy that doesn't require expert level mirror neuron function which can be difficult, if not impossible.[5]

5 Joe Biel, publisher of this here book as well as many others over the decades, happens to be autistic. In writing about Joe's own autism, Joe relates a story of doing film editing, and it was only the slowing down of video did Joe recognize these ever shifting human facial expressions even exist.

This is where I get out my secret therapist toolbox. A pragmatic and far more easily learned skill comes from Neuro-Linguistic Programming (NLP). I know that seems like a super borg name, like so many things developed in the 70s, but the idea behind NLP is that there are people people who do things really well, and we can model what they do in order to create change in our own lives, including in communication (the linguistics part of NLP). So NLP teaches a process called mirroring and matching that helps us get more simpatico with someone we are trying to connect with.

Mirroring and matching are processes in which we get simpatico with someone's body language and verbal language, which are way easier to notice and track than micro facial expressions. Mirroring refers to a process of reflecting someone back to them as if they were watching themselves in the mirror. Like if they cross their left leg and lean back, you cross your right leg and lean back. Matching tends to be a little looser and less immediate. If they take a sip of their coffee while you're talking and nod to show their listening, you may do the same thing once they are answering what you asked. Neither are meant to be mimicry, but instead operate as ways of hitting someone's wavelength so you vibe together. If you see people who know each other very well, you'll notice that they do this subconsciously. One person will take a sip of their drink, and the other person will do the same thing right after. And doing so consciously can help you demonstrate attention and attunement.

Mirroring and matching can include not just sharing body language (like leaning forward when they do) but also their tone of voice (someone who speaks softly and quietly, for example, will generally feel more at ease if those around them respond in kind), and even specific words that they use.

In therapy school, we break down attunement even further into reflection of content (showing we are paying attention to the story someone is relating by paraphrasing what they say to us) and reflection of feeling (showing we are recognizing the emotionality of the story, for instance by looking concerned when they are talking about something upsetting). We want to know that people *get* us, and these skills are a pragmatic demonstration that we do. If you struggle with dialing in to someone else's frequency, this will help you do so. And if you are great at being engaged but people don't realize that you are engaged, this skill will help you demonstrate the nonverbals that others respond to subconsciously.

Friendships Need Boundaries Too

The majority of work in therapy is work around boundaries. It's becoming more normal to think and talk about the boundary issues we have with family members and partners.But boundary issues within our friendships are still rarely discussed, even though they are just as important, if not more so.

If friendships in this day and age are generally the relationships we choose for ourselves then our boundaries should be co-created as part of that process. When we don't speak up about boundary violations, we often think this is in service of protecting a relationship, but that only works in the short term. Eventually we feel so shitty and overwhelmed we just dump people out of our lives . . . rather than giving them a chance to respect what is important to us. Being a better friend isn't just about respecting others' boundaries. Respecting and communicating your own is also a vital skill.

In my book *Unfuck Your Boundaries,* I defined seven different types of boundaries based on my clinical practice and how I think about relationship issues. Which is to say, I haven't done any factor analysis research on the topic or anything, just created a good working model to help people think about boundaries in a more practical way. They are: physical boundaries, property boundaries, sexual boundaries, emotional-relational boundaries, intellectual boundaries, spiritual boundaries, and time boundaries.

There is generally a lot of overlap between these categories, especially with friends. For example, the friend that really wants to borrow your Switch for the weekend might be bumping into a time boundary when they are running late to meet you, not just the property boundary of you not feeling great about handing over an expensive gaming system. A platonic friend who has been drinking and makes a handsy pass at you has just violated both your physical and sexual boundaries.

And maybe that complexity of experience is what makes the whole conversation so hard. It makes figuring out our boundaries and trying to communicate about them better so complicated. Because it high-key *is* complicated. But hey, as the author Glennon Doyle says *"We can do hard things."* And this is a worthwhile endeavor.

Besides having different types of boundaries, we also have the structure of the boundaries themselves to consider . . . which is more important than most people realize. Boundaries can be rigid, permeable, or flexible. While some people have set up camp in one of these categories, most of us will operate on a continuum of these in different situations. If we have permeable boundaries, we might just say yes to every friend who wants to borrow our electronics, and be very laid back about missing our doctor's appointment because they were running so late to pick it up. If our boundaries are super rigid, we might not only say no to the loan request but also send them an angry email telling them off for even having the nerve to ask.

While we don't want to let people walk all over us by keeping all our boundaries permeable, we also don't want to be such rigid stick-in-the-muds that we never learn and grow.

That flexible middle ground comes from listening to our internal voice that wants to protect us and wants us to experience growth. That's the voice that makes continuous calibrations about our boundaries, knowing that when we are willing to compromise in certain areas it may lead to the betterment of our friendships. Maybe you aren't comfortable with loaning out the gaming system you saved for months to buy. You also adore your friend and don't want to scream *"This is the first time I've ever been able to have an expensive system, stop trying to take things away from me!"* Flexible may mean "I'm still geeking out over finally being able to afford the system and not comfortable with my new baby going away on sleepovers, but I'd love for you to come over and we can order a pizza and game together. Or if you just wanted to test it out on your own, I'm working from home on Friday and you can hang as long as you want and fuck around with it, I'll be in meetings in the back room all day."

With all boundaries, we need the capacity to negotiate while still maintaining our safety and not becoming a total pushover or a total tightass. Flexible boundaries mean paying attention in a proactive way instead of reacting from old patterns. And that may mean you have to make some difficult choices. Because when it comes down to it, we either let the world dictate our boundaries for us *or* we communicate them with what we do and say. As off-kilter as it can be at times, I would *far* rather experience the discomfort of difficult conversations than let the world determine what is going to happen to me.

Boundary Violations

I've defined boundaries as the constructs that differentiate between ourselves and someone else. Boundary violations can occur when that space is not negotiated in conscious and mindful ways and our actions result in harm (regardless of our intentions). For instance, your friend asking to borrow your Switch probably isn't violating your boundaries (unless this is a whole thing between you and you've asked them not to try to borrow your stuff anymore), but if they badger or guilt you into saying yes when you've already said no, they might be, and if they pick it up and take it home without explicit permission, they definitely are.

This is very much about consent. Consent is used as a buzzword that confuses a lot of people, but in practice it's a simple concept. Consent is *the informed, voluntary permission given or agreement reached for an activity/exchange between two or more sentient beings*. When it comes to the expression and negotiation of our boundaries, we generally do so through how we communicate consent. If someone asks you "Hey, can I borrow this book?" they are recognizing that the book is something you own (property boundary!), and are asking for your consent to use it and return it. You are then free to give your consent, not give it, or give it conditionally.

Boundary violations are what happen when we act without consent.

Pia Mellody, author of *Facing Codependence*, points out two main categories of boundary violations. Her categories are, simply enough, external and internal.

1) *External Boundary Violations* are when people do something to you in a physical way. External boundary violations are tangible and measurable.

2) *Internal Boundary Violations* are when people violate your emotional space and try to get you to change your behavior and actions to suit their needs without requesting that change honestly. It's manipulative shit.

I tell people on the regular *"when we know better, we do better."* The big cultural shifts start with *recognizing* these violations. External boundary violations include things like touching people without consent, using their shit without consent, and not returning things on time even if they were borrowed with consent. Internal boundary violations include things like giving people unwanted feedback (no one needs to hear any criticism about their body, ffs), making judgements based on assumptions instead of facts, and sharing secrets and stories that aren't ours to share. Some boundary violations can be both internal and external, like jumping in and helping someone without asking and getting an affirmative answer that they wanted help (you aren't just physically jumping in, there is a presumed judgement about what they were capable of and/or needed).

Of course all of us have experienced boundary violations at the hands of friends. And all of us have violated the boundaries of a friend. And it's important to keep in mind that our brains are wired to do us dirty with something called the *fundamental attribution error.* When we mess up and violate someone else's boundaries, we attribute our actions to the situation at hand (whether this is a reasonable justification or not). When other people mess up and violate our boundaries, we attribute it to them being a fundamentally terrible person.

This is the brain's default way of thinking and until we develop an awareness of it and learn how to think through it, we can end up shitcanning friendships with perfectly great people who weren't really aware that their behavior was a problem. Adding a level of consideration and awareness allows us to pay attention to the details of each situation we encounter and make better decisions about whether someone is truly an asshole or just a blundering human that will do better in the future if we bring our issues to their attention.

Authentic Vulnerability

A big part of figuring out our friendship boundaries is figuring out the whens and hows of being vulnerable with our innermost selves. Vulnerability is defined as a state of being exposed to possible attack or harm. Maybe you front a death metal band but decide to admit to how much you enjoy the musical stylings of Debbie Gibson. Or maybe it's about letting people know more about your fucked up childhood and how you've struggled with your mental health as a result.

Lindo Bacon's book *Radical Belonging* devotes an incredibly thoughtful chapter to vulnerability in friendship. They point out that presenting our authentic self is far easier when we have privileged identities and personal histories that consisted of love and support. Meaning, sharing our trauma histories or aspects of ourselves that are not universally accepted (e.g., being queer, or poly, or a kinkster, or all of the above) and requires a level of trust that we won't be rejected for these differences.

There are a multitude of very valid reasons to not share our authentic selves with others. We may experience uncertainty, shame, or have a very real fear of retaliation. Dr. Bacon points out that we shouldn't judge anyone for self-protecting, and that includes ourselves. Many of us have gotten very good at putting on a friendly show, seeming engaged and open while still hiding the parts of ourselves that may be misunderstood or judged. It's entirely normal and valid to be careful about sharing certain things with certain people. Doing this at a professional conference is totally fine, but doing it around the people that are supposed to be our friends? That creates more feelings of loneliness and isolation than just staying home.

Which isn't to say that being the Overlord of Overshare is a better strategy. Brene Brown, the name we all associated with vulnerability research, discusses the overshare strategies that many people use in order to seek attention, energy, and validation from others. I've never met anyone who *intends* to be manipulative through an overshare dump but as Dr. Brown discusses, it still functions in the same way. The individual we are sharing with may not be ready or willing to absorb and hold space for the entirety of your story. Oversharing forces them into a dynamic where the expectation is they are able to take emotional care of us, and that's not what they had signed up for when they met us for a coffee date. The end result is that everyone involved feels more disconnected and uncomfortable. Instead of creating more intimacy, it created more barriers to achieving it.

As Dr. Bacon also shares, there are no magic glasses out there that help you spot the right people and no magic watch that tells you it's the right time, but they have found that it helps to try to stay grounded in the present moment and the present experience rather than pulling out the bag of stories they have created about their life. And it can help to wait for people to invite you into sharing rather than cannonballing yourself in. But it's also important to not put on an entire costume of a pretend-self which creates that feeling of performance rather than connection. We can engage authentically without sharing too much too fast. For example, maybe everyone is discussing their childhood and yours was un-fantastic. Responding with "oh, that's more story than we have time for at dinner!" sets a boundary without feeling like a performance or a falsehood, and also keeps the door open for that conversation to come up at a later time. And when we do reach that level of comfort and intimacy with others, we want to take care that it isn't a one-way street. Meaning we don't just unload all our shit and say "Thank you for taking on this hot mess, peace out!" But we also create space for them to share, should they want to. As in *"Okay, that was a lot . . . what's life been like for you lately?"*

Communicating Effectively

If boundaries are the scaffolding of our relationships, communicating about and around and through our boundaries is vitally important. Communication is not just about *the what*. In fact the *what* is usually the smallest piece of the puzzle.

Communication is about *the why*. Things are meaningful *because reasons*, right? Communication is the expression of why something is upsetting, problematic, stressful, wonderful, etc.

I think we often go into friendships with the thought that this is a relationship that we choose and this is someone who really loves us and gets us and is around us because they WANT to be. And that our communication will be intuitively understood because of the nature of that relationship. And there is probably some level of truth to that, but it definitely isn't a perfect system. And when that intuitive understanding radar fails I think we are extra buggered by it. We kind of expect our family members to not vibe on the same level as we are, but our friends? The people we choose because they are already on that level? We're far more likely to be hurt by mis-communication. We don't want to fight with the person who is supposed to be *our* person, and we tap out. But what if there was another way?

The late psychologist Marshall Rosenberg developed Nonviolent Communication (NVC) strategies as part of his extensive work as a coach and mediator in the 1960s. I've found his work to be exceptionally useful, and have incorporated it into other things I have written (pretty much every time I write about self-compassion). His communication model is a stepwise breakdown of the subtleties of both respecting our own boundaries and honoring those of another person, which is hugely helpful when we are trying to friend better.

Communicating Support

How do I support my friends? is a question I get asked *a lot*.

It's not generally the thing that brings people to therapy, but it frequently comes up as people start untangling all of the crap they are working to unlearn and begin to recognize that it has affected their friendships as much as it has affected their partnerships, their families, their parenting, their careers, etc. There are two main general communication struggles I see the most in friendships: figuring out what kind of support someone needs and figuring out how to maintain connection when things go really south.

What Does Support Look Like For Your Friend?

If a healthy friendship operates as a secure base, that means we not only feel good about being brave about goals and achievements, it means we have a relationship to call home when things fall apart. One of the biggest ways you can communicate that you are a secure base is the way you show up when a friend is going through something difficult. Your role is to find out if they are looking for **space**, **support,** or **solutions.**

You don't have to ask in those exact words. A go to question may be something like: *"Holy shit, that's a lot! Do you need to be left alone for some quiet time to process everything, or would it be more helpful for me to be here with you to listen? And I know you don't need anyone to fix your life, but if you want some help sorting out some options I can do that too."*

Now this doesn't mean that it's your job to sit there and listen for months on end to someone complaining about the same fucking problem while not doing a fucking thing about it. You can love someone dearly and want to preserve the friendship but be *very* over their complaints about their shitty boss week in and week out while doing nothing differently. There's nothing wrong with wanting sympathy while processing out loud and organizing your own plan of action. Or even when there is nothing much to be done but having someone else recognize that you are in a difficult place. But it's a far different thing when this is someone's modus operandi about life, and they seem to be gleefully wallowing in their misery and want you to bear witness.

This is where boundaries come in. You can lovingly tell a friend who wants to revisit the same issue where you listen and commiserate for ever and ever and ever that you aren't going to do that anymore. Something like *"I know we've talked about this a few times and I can tell you're really stuck. I think revisiting it is making things feel worse for you instead of better, let's focus on something in your life that doesn't suck or let's go do something together that doesn't suck so you have some kind of suck free zone in your life."*

They may have the type of personality that lends to dramatic responses and attention-seeking behavior. That doesn't make someone a bad person or a bad friend, just one that has learned to get their needs met in a way that is exhausting for those around them. And if you provide attention and support in a new and different way, they'll shift out of that mode far more quickly than you fear.

Or maybe your friend isn't a drama llama but they are legitimately stuck. Even so, the amount of venting another person can hear has its limits. When we are having a rough time, we need to express our appreciation and gratitude when people provide that sympathetic support, and then follow up with asking them what's going on in their lives. And we have to remember that our friends are not our therapists. They don't have the necessary perspective to give us that neutral view and it may be the kind of issue where finding a therapist or a support group would be more appropriate. It's totally okay to tell your venting friend, "this sounds like a lot . . . are you seeing a fancy professional for support or do you need help finding one that you can actually afford?"

And When It's Really Bad?

So this is about supporting a friend in deep grief and pain, the huge losses that affect all of us throughout life where we most need the support of others. I wrote about grief in my book

Unfuck Your Brain and spent a good deal of time writing about how to support others in deep grief, not just working with our own grief.

Part of what makes it so difficult to support others who are grieving effectively is the fact that we are so close to them. We feel awful with them, not just for them. And we are far more likely to smash boundaries in our attempts to feel better. For example, a friend may say "thank you so much for asking but there isn't anything I need right now and I really just want to hide out for the weekend." But we are worried about them and show up with a dozen cookies anyway. This isn't an intentionally unkind gesture and cookies are lovely. But they already said no thank you and our need to do something got in the way of respecting their boundary. But once we recognize that's our instinct, we can dial it in so we can be functionally supportive.

The best thing you can do is be helpful only when it's useful to your grieving friends, and not make it about your need to do something. That is, do things that help *them* feel better, not things that help *you* feel better. I always tell people *"If there is anything I can do that makes your life a little more manageable right now, please let me know. I don't need an assignment/something to do because I'm worried about you, but I'm your person for any task that you can't deal with right now."*

And you're thinking, okay but I have a hyper independent friend who won't tell me when they actually need help and I always find out later. And I'm *totally* that hyper independent friend. And my bestie has been wonderful at reminding me that he's there in those situations. If I mention something that didn't get done, he would say *"That's exactly the kind of thing I can help with, if you'd like me to."* No recrimination, just a reminder of support.

It's also hard, in these situations, to figure out how much space to give someone who is radio silent. A grieving person is generally not time-aware that they haven't reached out. And you don't want to be obnoxious about it but you also don't want them to feel abandoned. And praise be texting for giving us the perfect mechanism of support. This is where you say *"Hey, I was just thinking about you. I know you're going through it so you don't even have to respond but I just wanted you to know you were on my mind."* You can also offer low impact support, like dropping off food but not staying and hanging out and eating with them. Or dropping off a gift card for a restaurant they dig that they can use now or have as a resource later. These are small reminders that it is their turn to be supported and they don't have to perform any role in the relationship in order to receive that support.

Communicating Through Conflict

Friends have conflict. This is healthy and normal and means that you aren't a pushover. But in the thick of it, we often feel like it's the end of the world. Conflict can bring us closer together. But in the moment it doesn't feel like it, especially since most of us have had zero experience with the healthy expression of differing perspectives in our lives. But like everything else I talk about in this book, healthy conflict is a learnable skill.

To nod back to relational-cultural theory for a minute, I consider all of these topics to be falling under what Jean Baker Miller called *waging good conflict*. Dr. Miller was a huge advocate for staying connected through conflict by remaining compassionate (to others, and to ourselves) and by remaining respectful of others while keeping our own values, ethics, integrity, and boundaries to the forefront.

"Waging good conflict" refers to the process in which we move away from the more traditional Western models of conflict management (you know, someone wins and someone loses), many of which we learned within our own families growing up. Waging good conflict involves being open to listening to understand, not to respond. Which operates as a model that we hope the other person responds to, encouraging them to treat us with the same level of respect. RCT theorist Dr Linda Hartling frames this level of connection through the lens of human dignity. She states this isn't something that comes naturally from within us, but is co-created in relationships founded on respect and an authentic desire to understand those around us.

Please don't misunderstand me to say that this means you should tolerate truly awful and harmful behavior out of compassion. I think the reverse is true. If we are compassionate to others while remaining self-aware, holding our center becomes easier. We're far less likely to be manipulated because we are less emotionally bound up by someone else. We can maintain a respectful connection far longer. And we can detach, as needed, with love.

Nonviolent Communication is very process-focused, designed specifically to shift conversations to collaboration (which is *exactly* what we want in a friendship dynamic). Using relational-cultural theory means we are setting a tone of power-with another person instead of power-over.

Another focus of NVC is on language itself. Because it is very easy for us fallible humans to perceive the words of others as threats. Threats spur us into power-over reactions, meaning we are looking to win a fight, not to connect and honor needs and boundaries.

Dr. Dian Killian, an NVC consultant and coach, defines the four steps of collaborative communication as a way to express with authenticity and receive with empathy. Or, to use a more Dr. Faith-type verbiage? Generally speaking, people aren't out trying to act shitty. We are human, fallible, fuck-ups. And friendships are seen as the relationships that are easiest to extricate ourselves from, so we are far more likely to tap out than wage good conflict. Here's a super nutshell version of NVC:

1) **Observe/Review:** Listen to understand, not to respond. Then demonstrate that understanding with neutrality (meaning without judgement). "I heard you say . . . Did I get that right? Miss anything?" This helps prevent the conversation from getting heated, or at least from getting heated so fast. It's about reflection and clarification. Not "you're a fucking idiot because ..."

2) **Speak to your emotions:** There is a subtle difference between "I feel confused" or "I feel sad" instead of "I feel hurt" or "I feel disappointed" which can help open the dialogue further. Many people say "I feel . . . " then share an attitude, belief, or thought. Such as "I feel you aren't listening to me." NVC techniques also focus on the expression of emotional turmoil rather than emotional blame, as much as possible. This can be tricky when your emotional response is in direct relation to someone's behavior toward you. And this doesn't mean lie about what you're

feeling, but feelings are complex and bringing them to a more global position may help.

3) **Recognize the unmet need:** NVC founder Dr. Rosenberg felt that emotional turmoil existed in response to an unmet need. He identified eight universal categories of needs: autonomy, connection, honesty, meaning, peace, physical wellness, and play. So in this step, we are matching the expressed feeling to the unmet need. A friend seeming angry at you, may be struggling for a need for autonomy which may or may not even be related to y'alls relationship.

4) **Make a request:** This is where, after all parties are feeling heard and understood, a request that connects to the unmet need can be offered for consideration. Requests work best when they are positive and concrete. Even better when it is something that can be addressed immediately, not in the nebulous future. Requests in this paradigm are about what we want and not what we don't want. "Stop doing XYZ" brings out stubborn resistance in most everyone. And the word "request" is also important. Demands also awaken our inner toddler that screams "no" at everything. The

question I always get is "What if they say no? What if they say they can't commit to showing up on time when we have concert tickets?" And the answer is, they are telling you something about their relationship with you and you have a decision to make. If they don't honor your request, you have to decide if you can live with that or if that's a dealbreaker for you.

This is a more complicated process than some of the other communication strategies I have shared in previous books. And it's okay if it feels like a lot. Even just using the first step of the process can be incredibly helpful in working through conflict. And I can tell you as a person whose job is to communicate, and help others communicate, the rest of it becomes easier with time and practice and is an incredibly valuable skill.

Toxic Relational Strategies

The problems and conflicts in our friendships are probably mutual, but they probably aren't coming from the same place for each of us. In order to give each other the benefit of the doubt in our communication, we need to have an idea of where each other might be coming from. Because we have good boundaries, we can't work out our friend's shit, but we sure as hell can work on our own. A big part of that is figuring out what relational habits we may have formed in our lives that are no longer serving us.

These are *toxic relational strategies*, and they're a type of cognitive distortion that affects not just how we **think** in certain circumstances, but how we **interact** with others based on those thinking patterns.

A cognitive distortion is a thought we had that we decided to hold on to as a truth . . . even when it's not that true, and not that helpful. It's a story we've become attached to and act from. And it ends up causing problems. Typically when we read about cognitive distortions and common thinking errors, we are focused on the types of thought patterns that lead to a spiraling of depression and anxiety. But there are other kinds of thinking errors (and their accompanying behavioral patterns) that have just as large an impact on ourselves and an even larger impact on our relationships with others. Everyone has engaged in some of these strategies at some point in their lives. And we have all been victims of these strategies. Not just from perpetrators of abuse, but from otherwise good people who engaged with us in unhealthy ways because they thought that was the best way to meet their needs. The difference is in the degree in which we undertake them.

As you read this list, look at patterns of interactions in your own life, examining the toxic relational strategies that you were subject to as well as ones you have subjected others to. Paying attention to the bidirectional flow of these patterns is the first step in true change.

This list is based on research and training materials from multiple sources including the Safer Society Foundation, the University of Iowa, Moral Reconation Therapy, and my office partner (work wife) Brenda Martinez, who is a trauma-informed licensed professional counselor and licensed sex offender treatment provider. It is not intended to represent the totality of toxic relational patterns, but to start a conversation on how they affect your own life.

Anger as a Means of Control: When we use anger to control and manipulate the behavior of others. The difference between this kind of anger and impulsive anger is that the anger response is turned off the minute we get what we want.

Authoritarian Dominance: When we hold rigid boundaries and expectations that things be done "our" way.

Belittling: When we treat others (or their feelings, concerns, point of view) as comparatively unimportant.

Black-and-White Decreeing: When we term everything in extremes ("I can never trust women," or "All men are players.")

Blaming: When we place blame elsewhere or insist that others are responsible for our behavior. Also could be termed a refusal to accept responsibility.

Compartmentalization of Behavior: When we compartmentalize our behavior to keep from feeling guilty, to justify our actions, or minimize the seriousness of them. ("I only cheat when out of town for work, never when I'm home")

Credit Seeking: When we want credit for good behavior (Okay, I forgot to pay the electric bill and the power was turned off, but don't I get credit for paying the water bill and the Netflix?) or credit for extremes not engaged in (Okay, I wrecked your car . . . but I could have lied about it and said someone rammed into it while I was at the grocery store)rather than accepting accountability for behavior in question.

Criminal Pride: Feeling a sense of identity and accomplishment from hurting others. ("This is just how I am" or "This is just how I grew up.")

Diverting: When we change the subject to something more comfortable, intentionally redirect the conversation, bring up another problem, or intentionally miss the point of the conversation at hand.

Entitlement: When we think someone owes us something or the world owes us something because we are special, different, or have been through more than others have.

Fact Stacking: When we arrange facts in a way to explain our behavior, while omitting other facts that don't work in our favor.

Fairness Violation: When we believe that everyone is treating us unfairly and/or when we keep a mental scorecard regarding "fairness" in the relationship.

Fight Instigating: When we encourage others to fight, then we stand back and watch.

Frequency Minimization: When we minimize the behavior based on frequency. ("It didn't happen five times, it was three times at most!") This is a form of "playing defense attorney".

Gaslighting: When we deliberately obscure or twist facts to make others question their reality, memory, and ultimate sanity.

Grandiosity: When we make little things into huge, important things so we can shift the focus of attention.

Harm Discounting: When we insist that our actions did not cause the level of harm that others say they did ("I did it, but it is certainly not as bad as you think."). This is another form of "playing defense attorney".

Helplessness: When we act incapable or helpless and unable to do things for ourselves, needing others to do them for us.

Impulsiveness: When we can't wait for what we want and do not want to delay our desires, and pursue these desires at the expense of others.

Intention Denial: When we deny our intention for harm. It may be true that we didn't intend to be hurtful or didn't plan a way to control someone else, but that doesn't lessen the impact of our behavior and it is another way of diminishing our responsibility for our actions. ("I didn't mean it" or "Things just got out of control.")

Justice Seeking: When we punish or control others and frame it as punitive toward others because of their behavior toward us. This is another form of "playing defense attorney".

Justifying: When we justify our behavior so we don't have to take responsibility ("I wouldn't have hit you if you hadn't made me so angry).

Keeping Score: When we explain or **justify** behavior based on the past actions of others or ourselves ("I've always done more than you, so it's not a big deal that I didn't do what I said I would this week.")

Lying: When we intentionally state things that are not true, or do not include all details in an attempt to deceive.

Making Excuses: Similar to **justifying**, in that we use it to explain away our behavior rather than hold ourselves accountable ("I was depressed that day.")

Making Fools of: When we exaggerate the mistakes and weaknesses of others to intentionally demean them and lessen their voice and authority.

Minimizing: When we try to make a behavior seem like it has less impact on those around us ("At least I only made out with them and didn't sleep with them.")

Mind Reading: When we think we know what other people are thinking and make decisions based on these assumptions, rather than asking.

Ownership: When we feel a sense of ownership of other people, and feel entitled to control their behavior.

Phoniness: When we communicate and apologize insincerely, without fully taking responsibility and without intent to change (maybe just intending to stop getting caught).

Playing Dumb: When we act confused about a situation to avoid responsibility for our behavior, or continuously ask questions that imply we don't understand what others are communicating. ("What did I do? What's wrong with that? What do you mean by that?")

Projecting: When we presume what others are thinking, feeling, or doing based on what we are thinking, feeling, or doing.

Pushing Buttons: When we intentionally use information about another person to get them upset in order to distract from our behavior.

Secretive Behavior: When we hide our activities and omit information to keep people from knowing what we are doing.

Selfish Intent: When we think and act in terms of our needs only, and not the needs of others.

Self-Pitying: When we use statements decrying how bad we are in order to get attention paid to us ("No one cares about me" or "Everyone would be better off without me around")

Spiritual/Philosophical Bypassing: When we invoke religion or spirituality over personal responsibility in an attempt to ascribe different meaning to a situation or to avoid doing the work around uncomfortable emotions ("I'm just turning it over to God." Or "What does any of this mean at a constructivist level, anyway?")

Uniqueness: When we believe that we are unique in such a way that consideration of others (and sometimes rules and laws regarding conduct) do not apply to us.

Vagueness: When we respond vaguely or unclearly in order to distract from the truth or the content of the conversation.

Victimization Reversal: When we present ourselves as the victim in a scenario, rather than taking responsibility for our role in any events that occurred.

Wearing Down: When we continuously challenge others to give us what we want until they acquiesce out of exhaustion over the continued fighting.

Zero State: Feeling worthless, like nothing, a nobody, and/or empty inside and behaving in ways to help fill that void. This is often where narcissistic behavior stems from.

Questions to consider as you go through this list:

- Did you notice any patterns? Do certain strategies come up time and again?

- What strategies have you used on other people?

- Do you use different strategies for different people (partners versus friends versus family, for example)?

- What strategies were used against you in the past? By whom?

- What strategies are being used against you in current relationships? By whom?

- Are there any patterns that you notice in the strategies you use and the ones used against you?

- Are there any patterns that you notice in the strategies that have been used against you in the past and are being used against you in current relationships?

- What is one strategy that you have noticed in yourself that you want to commit to changing? How will you do so?

- What is one strategy that you have noticed in your current relationships that you are committed to no longer accepting? How will you do so?

Defriending

You know what sucks? Really fucking bad? Friendship breakups.

I am always touching base with friends, family, colleagues, and my online posse when I am writing on a new subject. I swear, I have never had such an immediate, hard-core reaction on a topic than when I asked for feedback on the topic of friendship breakups. In my therapy consultation group, everyone admitted that they had an immediate flashback to that one broken friendship experience the minute I asked. Why does this topic trigger *everyone*?

I think it comes from the cultural expectations and norms we have about friendship. When you think about it, we have far more realistic expectations about romantic relationships than we do friendships. And we have a way better handle on dealing with the fall-out when they fail.

As a general rule, most relationships don't last until death do us part . . . but there is way more pressure on our friendships than there is on our relationships. And when they don't last, we have no fucking clue how to deal. So what's the malfunction?

Friendship breakups are what happen when, for whatever reason, those ingredients for a healthy friendship are no longer there, we can't resolve the underlying issues, and we can't mutually meet our needs through healthy boundaries, communication, or waging good conflict.

Do You Really Need to Break Up?

Maybe your friendship is the over-ist over that ever over'd. But maybe not. Maybe you aren't sure what to do. Are you kinda going back and forth on this friendship breakup thing? Let's discuss.

First of all: Is it something they *did* or something they *are*? You know what I mean here. Are they fundamentally in a place that is dangerous for you in some way, shape, or form? Or did they just fuck up?

And when I say "just" I don't mean that it wasn't a big deal. Fuck-ups can be huge, nasty messes. But is it indicative of how they generally navigate the world and treat others? Or is it a genuine mistake or lapse of judgment? Is this an issue that has the potential to be corrected if it is discussed and new boundaries are established? If you were the one who fucked up, how would you hope people would approach you?

A lot of times we allow certain behaviors long enough that they become the norm. When we allow people to do certain things or treat us in a certain way, they are more than likely going to continue to do so until we stop them. If your friend is generally a good and excellent person and may respond to you setting new boundaries, it's worth trying to have that conversation before you go into break-up mode.

Or it may be that you can tolerate the behavior at a different level. For example, if you have the perpetually late/no-show friend who you otherwise dig, maybe only invite them to hang out when it's a group gathering where their arrival time won't impact festivities. Let them be their late-ass self on those occasions, but don't invite them to the movies.

If you still aren't sure if this is a break-up situation or a waging good conflict situation, ask yourself these questions:

Are you willing to make the first move on this?
Cuz we all fuck up. And sometimes owning our shit and apologizing is the most difficult thing ever. And we've all been there. Sometimes people will fade out rather than hearing uncomfortable feedback and making changes in their behavior.

Are you willing to start the conversation? For instance with that same perpetually late friend, you might say,

"Hey, I want to talk about what happened. I was really pissed off and confused when you didn't show up last week and then we haven't talked since. I'd like to talk about it if you are willing."

What is your friend's responsibility here?

What was the specific behavior that upset you? What was your response to that behavior? You want to frame it just like that.

"When you _____, I felt _____."

"When you were late, I was frustrated and irritated. I didn't want to miss the first part of the movie, but I had your ticket and didn't want to go into the theatre without you."

What is your responsibility here?

Is there anything that you did in this situation that you need to take responsibility for? Did you not establish or enforce your boundaries? Did you respond to your friend in a way that you are ashamed of or embarrassed about? Did you do or say anything that made the situation worse? Like . . . if there was a video playback of your behavior in this situation, are there any parts of the tape that would make you cringe?

"I realize I told you it was okay when I really wasn't okay with it."

"I realize that I screamed at you when you didn't show up, which was a shitty way of communicating my feelings."

What do you want to happen differently in the future for the friendship to maintain?

This is the other part of communicating effectively. After explaining what bothered you and how it made you feel, you want to ask for the behavior you want instead. "What I am asking for is _____."

"What I am asking for is that you text me beforehand to let me know if you're running late."

What will their role be in what you want instead?

You have requested a different behavior, now explain exactly what change this entails on their part.

"Is that something you are willing to do for me?"

What will your role be?

And explain your understanding of what your role will be.

"I know that I have responsibility here, too, and I want to make this better. In the future, I will talk to you about why I am upset without screeching like a sea monster the minute I see you."

So you tried the thing. Maybe eleventy times. Or maybe it was way not salvageable to begin with, and that's okay too. This is the part where you put on your grown-person pants and come up with a proper break-up plan. Because just leaving a break-up post-it note is a dick move.

How to Break Up

There are so many ways to break up with a friend, and none of them are any fun. Your method will probably be chosen based on the type and closeness of the friendship (like, you probably won't break up with a friend you interact with mostly at work in the same way as with a chosen-family-type best friend), the needs of the situation, and the reason for the breakup.

Leslie Baxter, a communications professor at Lewis and Clark college, asked college students about their relationship termination strategies. She collected 35 different ones, and organized them into 4 main categories. Her research, published in 1982, still holds up quite well today.

- **Withdrawal and Avoidance** – Basic ghosting. Just pulling away, avoiding contact, trying to let it die off on its own.

- **Intentional Manipulation** – Creating a hostile friend environment so the friend gets tired of your shit and dumps you.

- **Strategies of Positive Concern** – This is the *"it's not you, it's me"* convo. I'm not in a good place, I'm not good for you right now, etc., etc.

- **Open Confrontation** – Whether calm or explosive, calling out the ending for what it is.

So, of these types there are really only two that aren't dick moves if done right. Let's look at these options.

Withdrawal and Avoidance

Let's be honest, this is what happens more often or not. Since we don't have any real mechanism for friendship break-ups, we usually end up just passive/soft ghosting them out. It's not necessarily a total disconnect and freeze out. It can be not making actual plans, responding less and less frequently and with less and less depth.

This isn't always a dick move, actually. If it's a mutual agreement type situation, where you both just fade away from each other, no foul, it can be the best mechanism for dealing with the issue, especially if you have a shared social circle. You cool, it's not a *thing*, but . . . you grew apart and aren't really hanging out together anymore. It's cool if you both end up at the same party, you know? Not a problem. Just . . . you know how things go.

A really interesting 2011 conference paper by Sibona and Walczak on Facebook defriending noted that while friending is an active request and accept process, defriending isn't. They didn't study this particular part of the equation, but it did make me wonder if that makes the idea of ghosting out a friend feel easier and more acceptable at some level because social media has created a mechanism for doing so, at least for online relationships.

Oh, and if you misjudge this relationship as a fade-away and get called out for ghosting? Own that shit and apologize.

Open Confrontation

Sometimes? Sometimes just no. Sometimes you just can't even work this shit out, and they are not in agreement in the mutual fade-away.

Sometimes they end up in such a diametrically opposite place than you are that having them in your life isn't going to be healthy for either one of you.

But the slow fade isn't working. And manipulating them into breaking up with you, or pulling some "it's not you, it's me" bullshit is way too dick a move, for serious.

You have to be grown and have the convo. Pull up your grown person pants and do the things:

Tell them the reason. You don't have to be all bashing of their dickitude. But tell the truth, owning your response to their behavior. Remember, no one *makes* you feel a certain way. "Hey, Friend-Person? You have been partying hard lately, at least by my standards. You seem really happy and having fun, but it's not been something I'm comfortable with. I'm focusing on my job right now, and partying isn't good for me. I think at this point our lives are going in different directions, and maintaining a friendship isn't possible for me. I wish all the best for you."

Discuss the semantics. What are they? You don't want to see them ever again? You are fine to hang out at group events but don't wanna do bestie stuff anymore? What does this break up actually entail? "I know I'll see you at Steve's party in a couple weeks and I'm totally cool with that if you are, but hanging out one on one isn't something I want to do anymore."

Tell other concerned parties. But FFS, don't ask them to take sides. Tell them the facts and what your break-up entails. If you hear the rumor mill about your Ex-BFF trashing you, ask your peeps to cease spreading the word. "Not being friends with Ex-BFF has been hard enough, I don't want to make things worse by shit-talking them or hearing any gossip, but thanks for being worried about us."

Figure out how you want to deal with the social media aspect. I suggest the minimum necessary separation. It's already a big enough thing happening, right? If unfriending them makes life easier, let them know that is what's gonna happen. But don't do the whole blocking thing, unless they are dropping bombs all over your accounts and you really fucking have to.

Grieving an Ended Friendship

When my son was in high school, we were discussing the epic douchery behind shitty friendship breakups and I realized that what he is dealing with is no less mature than what I see adults dealing with on a daily basis (and have dealt with myself).

It just feeds into my best friend's theory that the human race is operationally still all in high school and if we could just get ourselves up to undergrad status we might actually be able to affect some real change.

I also asked my son how he dealt with friendship breakups. He said, in the way only a monosyllabic teenage linebacker can:

"I dunno, it like, takes a while. There's, like, stages . . . or something."

You mean like Elizabeth Kubler-Ross's stages of grief?

"Huh?"

Ugh, yeah. Nevermind, bro. But he's right. And he's smart, isn't he? He's never heard of Kubler-Ross but nailed it when he said that all endings have a process attached to them. We don't necessarily honor that in regards to friendship, but we *should*. So let's talk about how the stages of grief apply to friendship break-ups.

Denial: What? Nothing's wrong. They're just busy and whatever. We are as close as we always have been. Okay, I can see they read my text and didn't respond. But they will later, I'm sure. *Lalala*, we are *fine*.

Anger: Stupid ass. I'm awesome and they are a shithead. I'm going to tell them this. I'm going to tell everyone else this. I'm mad because (1) I'm hurt and (2) My expectations about this person weren't met. I feel raw and reactionary and all kinds of awful things.

Bargaining: This is the desperate and hurt part of us peeking out from behind the anger response. Trying to figure out how to hostage negotiate this system back into safety. Sometimes bargaining works to a certain extent. You cave on *your* values and relationship expectations in order to try to maintain a dying relationship. And end up feeling worse in the long run. Other times no matter what you do they are just *gone*, and you feel like a pushover for trying to bargain them back. Bargaining is a really normal impulse, though. It's our brain trying to create some homeostasis by snagging back what it feels is missing and necessary.

Depression: This is where the reality part kicks in. This person was your friend and you got dumped. And it hurts like hell. But there are no sad breakup movies for friendship. And Ben and Jerry's hasn't yet developed a flavor honoring our need to get fucked up on ice cream in our PJs because our bestie dumped us. Avoidance of this part of the process is where we cause ourselves the most harm, I've found. Own what you are feeling. Trying to quash it will make it fester. Breathing through it is how we best move on.

Acceptance: This is the part where the breathing doesn't have to take such *a fucking conscious effort*. It's not necessarily all better, but it's livable again. You are at a place where you know that it's done and you are letting go.

Here is the other thing to remember. The stages of grief thing is *not* a linear, step-wise process. It's recursive, and full of relapses. And remorse. And regret. And remembering.

Lots of RE words. *Re* is a Latin prefix that means "again and again." It's indicative of that cyclical way emotions and memories work. The acceptance stage isn't a magical place of all-betterness and calorie-free Nacho Cheese Doritos.

And that's okay. Nobody heals from a loss in a complete and logical way because human beings aren't wired to be like that. It's okay to think you are over your ex-friend and then find yourself with an urge to Facebook stalk them to see who their new bestie is. Or to try to reconnect and work things out.

Best thing to do when you are tempted to reconnect (or google them)? Take a deep breath. Acknowledge the serious missing going on and what you are feeling. But think about the following:

1) **What is the best thing that can happen here?** They realize that no one else loves them the same and they are miserable and will change their evil ways and be an excellent friend again?

2) **What is the worst thing that can happen?** You will see they don't give AF that you are not in their life anymore? That they will totally get back together with you and then treat you like shit all over again?

3) **What's the most likely thing that will happen?** And you know the answer to this, you totally do. Will trying to dig back into this relationship end in an emotional ass kicking for you? You know, *most likely*?

You are grown, and you can do whatever you want, of course.

But seriously, honey?

Don't do the thing. It's akin to putting your hand on a stove that you know is likely going to be hot. You know the getting-burned thing is gonna happen, don't you? Think of it as you would a romantic relationship that ended for the betterment of your emotional, physical, and mental health. Think of what you would tell someone you loved beyond all measure who was about to do something that would end up with them being hurt. You would do everything in your power to protect them, right? Because they are worthy of care and protection. And you are, too. Take care of your precious self the way you would anyone else you adore. And don't let a toxic friendship kick your ass again after you already escaped it.

The moving-on part is tough. Like all other forms of grief, this shit takes time. And you get to give yourself that time. And it's okay to reach out to other friends for support.

Remember a few pages back when we talked about the cultural expectations about friendships never ending and the lack of cultural ritual we have for letting them go?

The good part of that is that you get to create whatever grieving ritual or process you need in order to make your healing happen.

What do you need right now?

It's okay to be hurting, it's okay to grieve, and it's okay to ask for help. If you were in a terrible car accident, no one would tell you to toughen up. They'd bring you to the hospital immediately. Everyone needs care at critical times, but not everyone realizes what times are critical.

It's okay to identify what you need, articulate that need, and seek it out from others and from within yourself. That is what light shining through the darkness is all about.

I don't believe shitty things happen because the universe has some lesson for us to learn—that's an incredibly awful perspective on how the world works. Life is tough enough without ascribing to the idea that there are forces out there that are punishing us into submission. But? I do believe we can learn from sad and terrible circumstances. We learn about our own boundaries. We learn to recognize which people are good for us and which shouldn't be relied on in the future. And we learn to be kinder and more gentle with ourselves and others. None of these lessons make the pain we went through "worth it," but they do allow us the opportunity to grow in positive directions in the future.

Auntie Faith Answers Your Questions

F riendships are complicated and have so many very specific complexities. This is a big deal. This may be the deal that got you interested in the book. Like, all the sciencey stuff is interesting but how do you navigate your actual life? How do we be kinder to others? How do we connect? How do we read mixed signals in complex situations? How do we invite in rather than call out? How do we know when to hold a boundary or be more flexible?

It's also hard to write about these kinds of issues in generalities. We can discuss how we should handle certain things in theory, then real life shows up being all weird and janky and messy and we get thrown for a loop.

So I decided to lean into the weirdness and jankiness and messiness of real life and answer the actual questions that sparked the need for this book.

And also? If someone wants to pay tons of money for a fancy syndicated advice column I'm so in. The magazine I wrote for in the past folded years ago and that was a fun gig.

Dear Auntie Faith,

How do I make a casual friendship closer?

Good question! You can't, really. Not all on your own, anyway. But you can make room for a friendship to grow if the other person in the equation is also interested in doing so. And I think it is more than just a matter of setting up more hang time / friend dates. I would focus on doing and saying things that show you "get" your friend. That's the magical ingredient of friendships. This means paying attention to the smaller things about them and engaging around them.

Like, they mention their favorite cookies from childhood. And you see them at a grocery store and get them a bag. Or you remember their drink order, and pick them up one while getting your own on your way to meet them. Or the band they like is playing and you send them the show info link with a "!!! Should we go???" Not creepy obsessive details, but the little, kind ones that show you are listening and engaged.

Now, they may think you are a perfectly lovely person but for whatever reason don't want to have a deeper friendship with you. Try not to take it personally. I know it doesn't feel great when we like someone who doesn't feel the same way about us. But it generally isn't personal. They quite likely have shit going

on and they don't have space for anyone or anything new and
you can respect that even if it's a bummer.

Auntie Faith

Dear Auntie Faith,

In the last year, three of my friends have gotten married and five (!) have either had a baby or announced a pregnancy. I am so happy for them and I am ready to be flexible to maintain our friendships, but sometimes it feels like I have to do all the work to adjust to their new lives, schedules, and interests. Should I expect this to be mutual or is it all on me? What is your advice for maintaining friendships through big life transitions?

This is such a common issue, isn't it? I've had more than one client bring it up to me just in the past week. Which says something to me. Not that the newly hitched or the newly parenting people suck. And not that the uncoupled and child-free suck, either. But that our society structurally sucks because it makes these transitions so fucking awful. Community care and community fellowship just don't exist at the level we need it to in order to thrive in connection.

The traditional nuclear family is supposed to be what we aim for, but it's really not enough for anyone. Your friends are nuclear-familying right now, and chances are they are feeling disconnected, alone, and are struggling as well. Plus they have a tiny bawling human that looks like Winston Churchill barfing on them all the time. I remember those days and it's fucking awful. Not because babies are inherently awful, but the *aloneness* of new parenting.

Which isn't to say that you should jump in and babysit for them, or plan the wedding, or do anything that you don't want to do. But it is to say, we can shape our friendship groups into better communities of care that allow room and support for these big life changes . . . as well as room and support for any of us who opt out from taking them all. If marriage and babies lend to their lives being complete that's awesome. And if you are enjoying a complete life while either seeking those things or having no desire for them? Also awesome.

I don't know the details of what you are trying to arrange to stay in contact, but I can tell you that finding a sitter and affording a sitter is difficult and sometimes impossible. Your friends may be desperate for a kidless night out but are embarrassed to admit that they can't make that happen. Or they are pregnant and just exhausted from having to go to work and grow the teeth on a whole other new human in the process. Or they just got married and their work schedules are so weird they hardly ever get to see their spouse and want to see them, too.

When my kids were young, some of my friend group also had kiddos and some didn't. We generally went out Fridays after work, and focused on kiddo friendly spots. You know the ones that have a playground so the parents can have a frozen jack and coke in peace. Then when the partnered and parenting took off, the rest kept drinking or moved on to the next fun event on their list. It was very much a community of care solution. The structure supported everyone's ability to be present and no one felt the need to take on a heavier burden of planning or support.

If they're just exhausted, ask them if there is anything that might be a better option than going out after a long day of work, like watching movies together on their day off so they can grow teeth with their feet up.

Or if they are trying to prioritize their marriage, demonstrate that you respect them prioritizing their partner. Ask if they would like to bring their partner along or plan something another time that doesn't bump into their plans with their spouse.

And if you don't have any fellow unencumbered buddies to stay up late and do other stuff with? This is a good time to start expanding your friend group. It's nice to have people around who can take off for a camping weekend at a moment's notice or even just have coffee with you without checking with their partner about their schedule. The nature of all our lives is that things change and even good change includes some level of loss for everyone involved. There will be a continuous ebb and flow of people and connections to them in your life. It's worth fighting for the important ones, even if it will be different from here on out.

You def don't have to take on diaper duty no matter what,

Auntie Faith

Dear Auntie Faith,

How do you navigate a friendship where one friend has much more severe mental health needs than the other?

First of all, I love that you recognize your friend's struggles and behaviors as stemming from a very real illness. And that you are wanting to be kind and supportive in that process. At least that's what I am presuming about you. You didn't say as much, but I imagine if you just thought they were a shitty person you would have already tapped out.

We all have an expectation of relationships needing flexibility to be maintained over time. That we will take turns going through hard times and supporting each other through them. But when someone has a chronic medical issue (which a mental health diagnosis is), it can feel overwhelming for everyone involved. You don't want to be the perpetual supporter and caregiver and your friend would far rather not need a continuous level of support and care.

But the reality is that they do.

The good news is, this isn't your task to take on for them one-hundred-percent-all-the-time. They do have a *medical need,* which means they need treatment providers. Friends are friends, not treatment providers. I *am* a therapist, but I am not my friends' therapist, ya know? If they are having a hard time accessing care, that may be something you are comfortable helping them with but you can't take on their med management and safety planning and symptom tracking and the like.

And if that's the dynamic y'all have fallen into, it's okay to take responsibility for your role in it and step out. Say, *"I've gotten way too much in a professional role with you which isn't fair to either of us and isn't good for our friendship. Let's find you some mental health support so we can actually enjoy being friends."*

The other possibility in this relationship is not that they are over-reliant on you, but that they keep disappearing, canceling plans, and the like. They hit the wall of overwhelm and didn't show up for dinner or whatever. Also understandable. And understandably frustrating. And is worth having a conversation about so y'all can problem solve together. Is it that the stuff your planning seems like fun in theory but is too overwhelming in reality? Would they do better doing different stuff? I remember times in my life where my idea of hanging out with my bestie was to be burritoed up in a blanket on his sofa while he went about his day and occasionally handed me snacks. (Yes, he's amazing and no, you can't steal him from me).

Or it could be that they don't have a good handle on the flux of their symptoms and you may need to plan more loosely. Like, invite them to group stuff so if they don't show up you're not sitting alone somewhere. Or tell them to reach out to you when they have enough spoons to do shit and plan from there. That doesn't mean freeze them out in the meantime. Text them birb memes and tell them you love them, and remind them that you are down to hang when they are up for it, but let them be the actual decider. It removes the stress and overwhelm that you are both feeling while maintaining the connection.

And if you are the friend-person who is realizing your mental health needs have been on high alert for awhile now? Part of taking care of yourself is in recognizing and owning that. Let your friends know it's a lot right now. And that you are actively seeking support and care. I had a client years ago tell me that their impetus for starting counseling was the realization that he might be burning out his friends on processing what he was going through in his life. If you are asking your friends to hold space for you, first ask if they have the emotional energy to do so and respect if they don't. And if they are giving you love and support, make sure you reciprocate. If you end up making a verbal dump, end with something like "Enough about my crap, what's going on in your life?"

Auntie Faith

Dear Auntie Faith,

I started a moderately successful social media account and now it seems like everyone wants something from me. There are suddenly a lot of people who share my passionate interests and want to hang out but it's getting harder to make genuine connections. How can I tell the difference between people with real friend potential and people who just want to feel connected to this idea they have of me?

Hey friend-person,

I was listening to a podcast interview with pop singer Billie Eilish and her brother Finneas O'Connell (who is her co-writer/ producer/audio engineer as well as protective older sibling) recently and they talked about how now that her popularity is nuclear, her space is respected more than it was when she was just starting out. That "kinda famous" space that she lived in as she was coming up created a feeling that she was more approachable by fans, even when she was just trying to go out to eat with her family or whatever.

Our brains are wired for parasocial relationships, which means they recognize people that we engage with through media as people we know. These random strangers aren't being shitty, in their minds they really consider you a friend, as one-sided and inauthentic as that is in reality.

Which doesn't mean you can't make friends or other relationships with people that find you through some level of fandom. One of my favorite essayists, Sam Irby, met her wife on Twitter (which is an awesome story about the person who has a book entitled *We Are Never Meeting In Real Life*). But presumably Kirsten wasn't weird and demanding when she first contacted Sam, just a fan and a nice human and things grew from there.

Which is to say, if it feels weird and one-side and exhausting . . . it probably is all those things. I believe deeply in listening to one's gut.

If someone is kind, and excited, and non-presumptuous? Those are your possible people. Not the people who DM stuff like "Hey, will you read my manuscript" or "Can you help me with this issue," but the people who say "I love your content, and this article reminded me of you, I wanted to share it in case you hadn't seen it!" or *"Are you going to the ThingWeLoveCon this year? I'm going and would love to say hi if you're attending any of the same panels."* You know, messages that show reciprocity and a recognition of boundaries.

For everyone else, you get to flex your boundaries muscles by saying, "I'm at saturation point with projects right now, but thanks for thinking of me!" Which is also the perfect response for people who do seem genuine and might be an actual potential friend but you are busy and overwhelmed at the moment . . . all you have to do is add something like, "ask me again in a few months, though, it sounds like fun!"

And "no" is also a complete sentence,

Auntie Faith

Dear Auntie,

I'm in my early 30s and was diagnosed on the spectrum pretty recently. A lot of things about my life make tons of sense now. It's good to know I'm not a shitty person who doesn't deserve friends and relationships, which I thought was true for many years. But now that begs the question . . . how do I approach making friends with this new information?

Hey friend-person,

Friendship and neurodiversity has been studied far more in children than in adults, making it not greatly applicable to us, since kids have less complex social interactions than adults due in great part to their still-developing prefrontal cortices. And the limited research on neurodiverse adult friendships focuses mostly on men. So I don't have much research to stand on in this section, which actually makes it even more important to mention . . . since few people are doing so.

A likely part of the reason there is minimal research is that there is still the commonly held and patently false idea that neurodiverse people lack sociality (meaning they don't want to have friends and relationships) due to continuously disordered emotional states. So most of the research on neurodiverse individuals making friends focuses on social skills training in hopes that they can "perform" neurotypical friendship.

Social skills are useful for everyone, and if you are neurodiverse you are less likely to learn them by watching and modeling others' behavior (which is how we learn most of our day-to-day activities). My oldest definitely needed some assistance on recognizing and respecting the personal space of others, for example. You can always learn new skills throughout your life if you want to, and learning rules of etiquette, or how to read facial expressions are things you can find on youtube and in books if you are so inclined. These skills aren't about putting on a performance but about giving you more information.

However the idea that neurodiverse people lack sociality is patently false. Like you said, you actually *want* friends, right? The limited research out there shows that autistic adults view friendships in the same way as everyone else . . . as an opportunity to provide support and care to one another. And the idea that behavior with the people closest to us should be something performative rather than authentic absolutely ruins the entire point of making friends. One study of autistic adults referred to it as *coerced socialization*.

Friendship isn't a job interview, it's a place to be yourself in all your weird glory, neurodiverse or no. So it's no wonder that many neurodiverse individuals seek out spaces in which everyone else has a similar diagnosis and they don't have to worry about unwritten and spoken social rules, or need to be extra cognizant of their boundaries.

There is no magic answer to any of this, except for me to encourage my neurodiverse friends to not exhaust yourself trying to mask your diversity and to instead spend your energy on people who like and accept you for who you are. Choose friends who are willing to speak to their wants and needs directly and straightforwardly let you know if you accidentally step on their feelings.

And those of us who are not neurodiverse need to be kinder and *presume best intent* of everyone around us. One of the studies I read relayed an incident shared by a study participant who is an autistic woman. She noted that when a friend asked her if a dress made her look fat, her response was *"Don't be silly, your fat makes you look fat, not the dress."* Now, I would probably laugh hysterically in the middle of TJ Maxx if a friend told me that, but I imagine the story being relayed didn't go as well.

A good ally to a neurodiverse friend, even with their feelings hurt, could say "Okay, fair point. I was actually looking for feedback if this dress accentuates the areas of my body I like the best and doesn't look weird and lumpy in the back. And I should probably warn you that one of those unwritten social rules is that it's always safer if someone asks if they look fat to either respond "Not at all!" or "It's not a great cut for you, let's find you something else!" If we are presuming best intent, we are going to presume that the friend is not dropping some mean girl unkindness, but is legitimately trying to give helpful feedback.

Auntie Faith

Dear Auntie Faith,

Several times in the last few years I've had friends of varying levels of closeness suddenly pull back from the friendship with no explanation. Should I just let it go, or ask them what happened? What do I do when I'm the person putting up new boundaries or drawing back?

Hey friend-person,

Chances are pretty good that none of this has anything to do with you. Life is difficult. Modern life can be a bit of a hellscape. They may have been overwhelmed. It *is* also okay to ask the question, though. If you have unintentionally been a bit of a crap friend you want to know better so you can do better.

There is nothing wrong with saying, "Hey, I was just thinking about you and realized we haven't talked in a minute. I apologize if any of that is on me, either because I ghosted out without realizing or wasn't a great friend. I'm working on being a better person in general so I can take it on the chin if that's the case. If you have just been busy as fuck and it's not all on me, I can definitely relate . . . and holler at me when your head is above water again!"

They may not tell you, and you can't make them of course, but you definitely aren't getting any new info by silently wondering. But I have had these conversations with friends in the past and have had them go very well. Even if uncomfortable, it fell into the "waging good conflict" idea I wrote about earlier in this book. And the convos have ended on very good terms.

And what if it *is* your pull-back or boundary setting? The part of this book is on "defriending" in all its various forms may be helpful. For boundaries alone, I always advise truth as the best place to start.

You can tell someone, "I've been kinda shit about expressing my own boundaries lately and I need to get better at it. It's not your fault for wanting me to stay late at the party, it's mine for not saying I was really ready to tap out. I'm working on getting better at that so thank you for respecting me flexing my 'no' muscle around you more!"

It's super hard to get defensive at a statement like that, right? You're taking it as yours *and* setting up the expectation that they will respect your boundary-setting in the future. And if they don't? Then you have a decision to make about this relationship.

Auntie Faith

Dear Auntie Faith,

I have in the last year become super close with one of my close friends. So close that I think we are starting to fall into dysfunctional family roles with each other. We know each other so well that we can trigger each other without even realizing it. How can we make sure this close friendship stays healthy? Or I don't get cancelled like her father?

Hey friend-person,

Auntie is so proud of you for realizing this yourself! You know that most people don't notice that they are repeating relationship habits over and over throughout their lives until it is their time to step on a rainbow. Science writer Lydia Denworth, in her book *Friendship: The Evolution, Biology, and Extraordinary Power of Life's Fundamental Bond,* stated that you can't understand friendship without understanding relationships in general, which is why attachment theory research keeps popping up like mushrooms in swampy weather.

And this is another of those situations where the best course of action is to own what you think may be happening. In the vein of, "It hit me like a ton of bricks recently that as much as I recognize my family was dysfunctional as fuck, I still fall into those dynamics. Short version? I think that I've been acting like my mom in ways that are pretty similar to how your dad treated you. And I know you ended up cutting your dad out of your life for your own mental health, so I don't want that to happen to us. I want to be better at just being your friend, not acting out family bullshit scripts that aren't good for our mental health."

I know I keep harping on taking responsibility for what is yours and not focusing on what is theirs. I do so for several different reasons. The first is that people don't resist change, but they resist being changed. Most everyone doesn't do well hearing about themselves until they are ready and open to that conversation. If you own what's yours, that becomes an invitation for self-reflection for your friend. But you can't shove the mirror in front of them, they gotta do the work of being ready. Also? Fundamentally the only thing we can control is ourselves. The only person who we can ensure respects our boundaries is ourselves. The only behavioral change we can enforce is our own. But our own work changes the system. Tapping on one part of the web makes the whole thing vibrate. You doing your part, whether or not they consciously do the same, may be all it takes to snuff out the toxicity.

Auntie Faith

Dear Auntie Faith,

A friend recently gave me a gift that revealed that they hold our friendship much more closely than I do. In fact I am worried that I am their best friend or even their only close friend and I don't feel ready for that kind of responsibility to them. If this was a romantic relationship there would be a conversation for us both to opt-in to dating. But there isn't really a script for friendship. How can I draw these boundaries more clearly?

Hey friend-person,

The tough thing about this is the fact that we don't know what your friend's intent really was. Some people are consummate gift givers. They get really excited at finding the perfect present for someone and it's really about the joy they feel in doing that. I'm one of those people, so I try to preface it with, "This may be a little much, but I got so excited when I saw it, I just had to be a little over the top and get it." I've chatted with my fellow gift savants about it, and everyone I have talked to feels the same way. We just really like getting awesome presents for people, it isn't about any expectation in return.

And it's okay to graciously accept the gift. And even if it is tied to how strongly they feel about you, it's also okay for them to consider you a very dear friend even if you don't feel the same about them. And you don't have to perform best-friendship for them, if that's the case. Like you said, maybe you are the only person they feel close to for whatever reason. And that's valuable to them. You can still set boundaries about your own availability and explain that you don't have the bandwidth for certain interactions. It is pretty similar to one person having a crush and the other not reciprocating. You mentioned there's a script for that, but really only sorta. If someone asks for more than you want to give in any respect, it's up to you to set the boundary and up to them to decide if they are fine with the level of relationship that you are available for.

I love that you are worried about them, and want them to have a bigger social support system. You give a shit and don't want to let them down. And if you want to include them in activities that may help them expand that network, that's great. But you aren't required to do so. And whether they do expand their circle, with or without your help is ultimately up to them.

Auntie Faith

Dear Auntie Faith,

When I got married my best friend started acting jealous. Help!

Hey friend-person,

True story, I refer to my bestie as my other husband. And he had zero problem telling my actual husband (Mr. Dr. Faith) that he was here first and could disappear Mr. Dr. at any point he saw fit. Bestie and I have a history together that no one can replicate. Mr. Dr. respects the hell out of that and they get along famously and will even hang out together without me. Which is to say, when I married Mr. Dr. Faith, he folded into the family I had created for myself with my friendships. Bestie and my son were the ones that gave me away at our wedding. And while we don't spend the same amount of time together, Bestie and I both know we are always there for each other, love each other, and do prioritize hanging out together, supporting each other, and texting academia chisme back and forth.

So I guess my question is, in what way does your Bestie feel left out? Is it the physical amount of time, which honestly ebbs and flows just because life happens regardless of partners being on the scene? Or do they see themselves as deprioritized? Are you cancelling plans with them because your spouse wanted to do something else? Are they out of the loop of what's going on in your life?

Are none of these things true so far as you know but they still feel the vibe is off? The only way to find out is to ask them. And hope they answer truthfully. Then y'all can plan for time together that is nourishing for your friendship . . . because that nourishment will be good for your marriage as well, it's not just about placating a grumpy buddy, right?

And if they say everything is fine when it is clearly unfine? Just nod and respond with, "If that ever changes, I hope you know you can tell me. I always want to hear the truth, because you're one of my favorite people in the world," and then let it go.

Auntie Faith

Dear Auntie Faith,

I have a terrible memory for things people say. This means that my friends often expect me to remember important facts they've told me about things like relationship status, food allergies, their health stuff, etc and I feel horrible for not remembering. Or worse I never really absorbed it to begin with. How can I be a better friend without exposing myself as a shitty confidante?

Hey, friend-person?

I'm super curious why so much info is slipping through the cracks. I can totally get not remembering if your friend has a pecan or walnut allergy (and double checking before throwing either one into the dinner salad) but not remembering their relationship status seems pretty big and makes my diagnostic brain wonder if it is indicative of a bigger issue.

Specifically, I'm wondering if you are neurodiverse or struggling with some kind of medical condition that is creating big problems for you. Do you struggle with details in other places as well? I say that not to be snarky, but out of genuine concern. If you were a new client in my practice, I would want to screen you for TBIs and ADHD at the very least. If something clinical is going on, you could benefit from support and treatment in multiple areas of your life.

Putting that caveat aside, whether there is a missed diagnosis or not, some kind of memory support tool will be of benefit to you. Way back as a undergrad psych student, I learned about *Farley files*. James Farley was a total political animal. He was Franklin D. Roosevelt's campaign manager and went on to be both the Postmaster General and chairman of the Democratic National Committee. He kept a file on everyone that both he and Franklin D. met. When people were scheduled to meet with either one of them again, he reviewed their file. So he could walk out and say "Ben! Good to see you! How are Rosie and the boys? Did Ken choose a college yet? You must be so proud! Remember last month when you were here and suggested I touch base with Wendell at the state department? Good call, he was so helpful!" Blahblahblah, etc.

One of my assignments in my industrial-organizational psych class was to choose a topic for a Farley file and create a sample. I made extra money doing a little catering as an undergrad, so I created my Farley project around that (hates almonds, allergic to dairy, the cake for the Christmas party was a huge success, etc.). It was a good way for me, as someone with a pretty great memory, to recognize that it isn't perfect and that keeping notes of important shit is a worthwhile endeavor.

Now this was the early 90s, so our Farley Files were literal files (I think mine may have been index cards for space-saving). But now we are all walking around with little computers in our pockets, so keeping notes in your Notes app is pretty easy, and referencing it on the fly also becomes easy. And maybe after some built in don't-forget strategies you will realize that you are retaining these details pretty damn well once you start flexing that muscle.

Auntie Faith

Dear Auntie Faith,

Sometimes a friend will drop a super personal detail in conversation casually and then move on. When is it too late to come back around to ask them about it or to even figure out if they want to talk about it?

Hey friend-person,

I asked my brother why he and I never had the big coming out convo and he shrugged and said "We didn't need to. You weren't gonna have questions or concerns. I didn't have any worries about who I love meaning something different to you about who I am. The more important question is where are we going for breakfast tacos?" And maybe your friend's truthbomb was meant as pragmatically as that.

But I appreciate that you are worried that you left some vulnerability hanging and want to check in. Kinda like I asked my brother, "Is this a convo we should have or nah?" I don't think it is ever too late to say "Wait, what?" about something important. I would reach out and say, "It's been a minute, but I realized at lunch last week (month, year) that you mentioned XYZ was going on and I dropped that thread. Was that something you wanted to talk about or just something you wanted me to know? I'm absolutely available to hear more about that if you want to, but I am also very adept at eating a big slice of shutthefuckup cake and not saying another word."

Auntie Faith

Dear Auntie Faith,

My friend sometimes makes comments that are frankly kinda bigoted. Should I call them on it? How?

and

Dear Auntie Faith,

If you haven't talked to a friend in a while and then when you reconnect you've ideologically drifted away, what do you do? Do you confront them? Let it go? Is it even worth maintaining the friendship? It seems weird to maneuver yourself into a position to be their educator—that seems to blur the roles of friendship.

Hey friend-people,

I'm answering these two letters together because while there are some differences, the general question is the same: What boundaries do I set up and what role do I take on with people who are, theoretically, friends but are also kinda acting like assholes? And especially if their assholery is the kind of thinking and behavior that is leading to a lot of the problems we are having in the US specifically and the rest of the world in general right now.

First of all, I'm always curious how this is presented. Bigoted in what ways or ideologically different in what ways? Is it "I don't understand gender fluidity but whatever floats people's boats?" or "I think people who are nonbinary are mentally ill and need conversion therapy?" Is "I think we should focus on infrastructure concerns in the city before we expand the Pre-K program" an ideological difference or are we talking more about "I think we should outlaw critical race theory being taught in any classroom because I read on Twitter that it's Marxist"?

Which is to say, there are disagreements to be had that are not about the dehumanization of others. I recommend Sarah Schulman's book *Conflict Is Not Abuse* as a good resource about connecting with empathy in ways that can change hearts and minds. The strategies of nonviolent communication are also designed for just such dialogues.

And of course you are not required to engage in any such dialogue. Especially if you don't have an ongoing friendship with this person. If you haven't talked to someone in ten years, you find each other on Facebook and you think "ugh, no" you can poltergeist right back on out. And no one is required to be anyone else's educator.

But changing hearts and minds and learning to see the perspective of others is most likely to happen in dialogue. Not in a powerpoint presentation telling them why PreK is a far more needed program than pothole filling. But in conversations like "Oh! I see why that's important to you, my experience has been very different and I've been very invested in XYZ for ABC reasons!"

There are also many people out there who are incredibly lovely and kind and don't know that their viewpoint is problematic. There is a reason that issues like racism are best conceived as not being the shark, but the ocean that we are all swimming in. Pervasive problematic issues are so ingrained we just stop seeing them. I've had conversations over the years with people, pulled aside or in a private message where I've said things like "I only know you as an incredibly kind hearted person, and I know you would want to know how I took your comment as someone with a different background" . . . and then lay it out. And see if they can sit with the discomfort of a different perspective and accept it. Auntie is biracial but light enough to be passing(ish), so she hears things on the regular that are . . . fucked up. And has no problem telling people so. And has generally found that when this is communicated in connection they really do accept it and make changes. Yes, that's a lot of relational labor. But that is also how we change the world.

Auntie Faith

I met this great person and we really hit it off. I got really excited, but after the first couple of dates she said she just wants to be friends. I know she's entitled to want what she wants and of course I won't pressure her. But the problem is that this is what happens every time I meet someone and there's a spark. That means that now I have a lot of friends who are cool, smart, hot women, but I still really want a girlfriend. Help! Is it something I'm doing wrong? Am I choosing people who are unavailable? Are my expectations all wrong? How do I meet someone great and make it stick?

Hey friend-person,

First of all? Props for taking being friend-zoned on the chin. So many people treat it like it's a bad thing. Like you are somehow a simp for accepting a different relationship from what you were hoping for. And props to the ladies you are going out with for telling you exactly how they feel without leading you on or ghosting you out. It takes courage to say "I like you, but not like naked sexitimes like you." And it takes courage to say "Bummer, but I like having you in my life as a friend-person if not as a naked sexitimes person so I want to stay in contact."

I don't get any kind of vibe from you that you are hanging out with these friends hoping they will see the error of their ways and fall in love with you and are seething that you are "wasting your time" in the friend zone and they are somehow taking advantage of your niceness. So many people have taken on those toxic cultural standards that someone who goes out with us somehow owes us something, which is clearly untrue but there is a big chunk of the Twitterverse that strongly disagrees and has no problem yelling about it. Your grace in these situations is much appreciated by your friendly, neighborhood sexologist here.

So as for the finding-an-actual-gf advice? First off, keep doing what you're doing. If you are using a dating app, recognize it's a numbers game. A rejection is not a rejection of your personhood but of your offer. It's called dating not girlfriending for a reason. "Thank you, next" is part of the process, even though it's crappy when it happens. If you want a girlfriend, one isn't going to be delivered to your doorstep so you have to keep being vulnerable and putting it out there.

Also? You have a group of amazing friends-who-are-girls who can now be enlisted to help you out. Let them be your wingwoman when y'all are out and about. Most people are terrible at reading cues of interest directed at them, but a friend will notice. Ask them to go up to people who they notice eyeing you and say "Hey, that's my friend-person. We aren't together but they are an amazing human. If I read you correctly as checking them out, I will 100% give you their number to you because I bet y'all would hit it off."

And they can wingwoman in other ways, too. Ask them! If you say "I'm not trying to present a fake self, but I want to demonstrate my *best* self when meeting someone new, what do you think would help?" Maybe they'll help you fluff your dating profile up a bit. Or help you shop for a new look that makes you feel comfortable and confident. Or maybe they know someone who is as big a Star Trek trivia nerd as you and wants y'all to meet. This isn't the same thing as sobbing *"Why didn't you loooooooove me?"* which would put them on the defensive, right?

With creativity and time you will eventually stick the landing,

Auntie Faith

Dear Auntie Faith,

Help! I have developed a massive, raging crush on my best friend. They have never shown the slightest interest in me that way. I don't even know if they're queer. I'm scared that if I say something I'll ruin our friendship. What should I do?

Hey friend-person,

I was super curious if there was any studies on people who have gone from friends to relationshipping, and it turns out that there is. And the research doesn't bear out well for the hopeful crushing. Some researchers looked at longitudinal data from PROSPER collected by researchers funded by the National Institute on Drug Abuse and the National Institute on Alcohol Abuse and Alcoholism. The study was on het relationships, which doesn't relate to your situation in the same way, but it was a huge sample of how friend groups operate. Friendship means proximity, right? The researchers wanted to test if proximity informs a transition from platonic relationships to romantic ones.

And the answer was: pretty rarely.

So in *My Best Friend's Wedding* when Julia Roberts decided that she wanted to convince Dermot Mulroney to marry her instead of Cameran Diaz because they had been friends so long? And he was all "Um, no"? That is the far more likely real-world outcome than what most movies show us.

This isn't to say it doesn't happen or won't happen. But since you mentioned that they have shown no hints of any interest in you it's probably more likely that you are gonna be the Julia in this situation.

This doesn't mean you can't gently test the waters or even ask outright. There's nothing wrong with either. An outright ask is a courageous one, because it requires a larger level of vulnerability and trust that friendship can withstand a possibly uncomfortable conversation. They can and do.

But if that feels like too much? A gentle test convo allows for authenticity without all the rawness you are feeling anxious about. Something along the lines of, "I know we're not like that, but you are exactly what I'm looking for in a partner so if you ever run into another you that would be interested in dating me I demand an intro!" That allows them to laugh and say "You got it!" or "Hey, I would 100% be into dating you myself!"

Either way you have the info you need to move forward, right?

Auntie Faith

Living in a west coast city where polyamory is a pretty normal thing, how do I make it clear to a potential friend that we are going on a friend date and not a date-date? Casually mentioning that I have a spouse is not effective here. Hilarious awkwardness ensues.

Hey friend-person,

This is super interesting to me! While I live in the deep-ass south not the progressive West Coast, I do know and hang out with lots of polyam peeps. I mean, aside from being a sexologist I tend to like interesting people who flout social norms. But even with that being the case, I've never had a polyam bud presume a sexual level of interest on my part. I've definitely been flirted with, and respectfully asked if I'm interested ("Hey I know you're married, but if you are ever interested in taking on a play partner and Mr. Dr. Faith is cool with me in that role I'd love to do something with you"), but noone has tried to hump my leg without first asking permission. Maybe because I also teach consent courses?

You have a couple of options here: a straight-forward one and a more subtle one. Both can be approached with humor and lightness, however. If straight-forward (or queer-forward as the case may be), I'd caveat with something like "Not to overestimate my pure raw sexiness or anything, but I've had a couple of people invite me to hang and I missed that they thought it was a date-date, and they assumed that my partner and I are poly. I didn't get that vibe from you, but I wanted to make sure this is a friend hangout, not a plan for sexitimes."

More subtle could be something along the lines of "Apparently my number has ended up on some swinger club bathroom walls, because the last couple of people I hung out with presumed we were on a date and didn't realize my partner and I are monogamous. I love being able to hang out with someone who doesn't think otherwise!"

And then maybe everyone who is presuming otherwise needs to take a consent class,

Auntie Faith

Dear Auntie Faith,

I've been hooking up with one of my friends for a few months. We've agreed not to tell anyone else in our friend group. The sexy times are fun but I feel more and more guilty that we are keeping this big secret. And there's nobody I can talk about it with. Am I going to screw everything up and end up friendless and alone?

Hey friend-person,

First of all, is the secrecy part of the fun? It generally is. At least at first. If that's part of the dynamic for y'all and the guilt is more theoretical than real (meaning do you think you *should* feel guilty or do you actually feel guilty?), then go forth with your sneak-snocking. Sure there could be consequences, but that's true of all the things. Unless y'all have other partners at home that don't know about your shenanigans it's not shitty behavior to keep your business quiet.

If the guilt is more real than theoretical then my question is what is activating the guilt? Is it because keeping things from your friends feels like a dick move? Or is it because you're catching feelings and want to make the friend-to-relationship leap with your hook-up bud? If it's the latter, you need to talk to them first no matter what. If you're in your feelings and they want to keep it as it is, then you need to step away from sexitimes before you get *really* fucked up. If they are like "yeah! Let's go public!" then y'all put on your grown person pants and say, "Hear ye, hear ye . . . announcement . . . we were kinda fucking around and kept it quiet because we didn't think it was going to go anywhere. But it did so y'all deserve to know what's up . . . we know that kinda makes it weird but we are going to do our level best to maintain the vibe we've always had. And if this doesn't work out we are going to do our best to not put any of y'all in the middle of anything cuz that's uncool and unfair."

And honestly? Even if you just want to be upfront with everyone because you suck at keeping secrets? A variation of the above totally works, you're just leading with "We've been kinda fucking around and had been keeping it quiet because it isn't serious but the lies-by-omission thing felt icky to us, and y'all deserve to know what's up . . . " then carry forth with taking responsibility for not putting people in the middle of whatever y'all are doing.

Either way, your friend with benefits needs to be on the same page that this convo is going to happen. If they vehemently disagree about it getting out there and you want to do it anyway? That's your choice but still let them know it's happening before it does so they aren't blindsided.

Alexa, Play "Truth Hurts,"

Auntie Faith

Dear Auntie Faith,

I'm newly single. My ex and I agreed to "stay friends" but every time we meet up for coffee I come away feeling terrible. They were so important to me for so long and it feels wrong to just kick them out of my life. But I don't feel this way around any of my other friends. Is post-breakup friendship possible?

Hey friend-person,

This feels like one of those situations that is designed to "prove" if we are cool and evolved, doesn't it? Cool and evolved people can be totally okay with being friends with an ex. Cool and evolved people don't shut other people out of their lives just because circumstances change. Except? Sometimes it feels like a fucking punch in the gut to see the person you expected to spend the rest of your life with and that is no longer the plan.

And it doesn't matter who did the breaking-upping. Or how mutual and healthy it was. If y'all were together for a minute, you need grieving time. Cool and evolved people are still allowed to be sad. I think it's entirely possible to be friends with an ex. But all those leftover relationshippy feels need a chance to wither off. You may need to take some space to do that work and then reevaluate. And even a few months from now you may need to set some limits around your interactions. As in, you don't want to hear about their new sexitimes with other people. Or what's up with their friends that you somehow lost custody of in the breakup.

It's also okay to *not* be cool and evolved. Even after you take some break-up grief space. You definitely should minimize contact with any ex that was toxic, abusive, coercive, or boundary violating to whatever extent is possible. But you don't owe any level of relationship to any ex, no matter how perfectly nice they may be. Some people just don't do well with that. It's totally okay to be politely distant. To nod and say, "Hey, good seeing you!" if you're at the same bar and then go back to your own fucking life and whatever you were doing that didn't involve them. It doesn't make you a bad person in the least. It does make you one that knows what you need for your own emotional health.

Take care of you,

Auntie Faith

Dear Auntie Faith,

I briefly dated someone years ago and we've stayed friendly. Recently he has begun to barrage me with multiple messages a week. Links to articles that interest him, photos of things he's observed in his daily life, updates about his health. Never once has he asked how I am doing or said why any of these things make him think of me. It's gotten really frustrating. I'm open to being friends with him but how do I tell him that this is not the way to go about it? I've stopped responding but that hasn't slowed him down.

Hey friend-person,

Your ex is pure COVID-19 energy, isn't he? I think that when we are disconnected, isolated, adrift, alone, fearful, etc. we tend to reflect back on our lives and connect back to times and the people from them that help us feel more hopeful and anchored. We do that anyway, and the COVID-19 pandemic created a perfect storm for those feels. Which doesn't make him a bad person, but he is being an inconsiderate one.

You can go about it a couple of ways. You can respond to one of his texts with an opening to ask how you are. Like "that's a gorgeous flower, a nice thing to see during a tough week!" and see if he recognizes that two people exist in a friendship and you aren't just a support bot. If Captain Oblivious still doesn't get it, you can get concrete as pavement. As in "Hey, I'm glad after a sad breakup we have been able to remain friends, but friendship is a two-way street. Which means asking about how I am doing and listening to the answers, not just sharing your own stuff with me."

And then send him the Nonviolent Communication four step model for listening. If he *still* doesn't get it? He's a total toad, and Buddha bless that y'all aren't a couple no more. You have my permission to continue not responding or to put his number on DND or just block it entirely.

It's also pure COVID-19 energy to not put up with bullshit anymore,

Auntie Faith

Dear Auntie Faith,

I have an easy time making friends and have always made friends with coworkers. Recently I was promoted, though, and now I am the boss of several friends, including one who is a little bit of a slacker. That never bothered me before but now it's my job to hold them accountable. But when I try, they don't take it seriously. Help, how can I keep my friend and also do well at this job?

Hey friend-person,

Ugh, this sucks. Been there. I got promoted and my two work besties had entirely different responses. One (J) took it to step up and support me. And the other (R) was furious that my promotion wasn't his license to fuck off even more than he was. And what made the whole thing a total shit show was this was community mental health. And his slacking meant the clients we served weren't getting appropriate care. If our job is to make subs and you're smoking weed behind the dumpster when we are cleaning up for the night I'm not gonna give two shits. But if you are fucking over *people*? Who need our *care*? I will end you.

You can def try having a conversation about why you are on them to do more better. If you go in with the vibe of *"My job is to support your ability to do your job and that's true of everyone on the team . . . this isn't about me being a tattle-tale in a company that already makes balls money"* you might get somewhere. If you explain that their fuckery is making other people's lives harder when y'all already have enough shit to contend with, you might get somewhere. What is the end result of their behavior? Are they willing to be grumpy but modify as to not fuck over other people who also hate their jobs there? And if not, start documenting and be ready to let them go.

If your job means protecting and supporting the people working for you and they are getting in the way of that? Nope, gotta go. And anyone I ever fired really fired themselves because of egregious behavior and I sleep just fucking fine over it. J talked to R who remained peeved and shitty. And I talked to R who still remained peeved and shitty. So guess what?

I fired his ass and changed the locks on the building,

Auntie Faith

I'm from another country, so frankly I find the whole concept of work friends a little weird. We don't really do that where I am from. Not that people are cold, but work is work. Then you go home or go out and that's where your friends are. Am I over-politicizing American work culture by thinking that the idea of work friendships is another way of reinforcing that our identity should be tied to our jobs and careers? I'm not trying to start shit, but it seems systemically sus to me.

Hey friend-person,

It does seem sus, doesn't it? And I happen to agree that tying our identities as humans to our paid labor is shitty and cruel. It's also been good for the care and maintenance of billionaires so of course it's a reinforced system. Although when you look at the research about work friendships, it is generally the *bosses and managers* who think they are a bad idea. So much so that the Gallup research peeps have caught shit for asking about work friends.

So the Gallup researchers wrote a very subtweety blog post explaining that they ask because it's important. Not just because work friendships are beneficial to employees, but they are also beneficial to employers. The people with work friends were more productive, less likely to hurt themselves on the job, had happier customers . . . and made the company more money. So it is actually a win for capitalism as well.

Now, I feel you on not owing the system anything more than the tasks you are being paid to complete. That being said, it doesn't mean that having work friends ties you more tightly to the company itself. I think for most people, the work friendships help buffer the bullshit and can be a useful part of getting through a crap shift. A Rand research study demonstrated that 1 out of every 5 employees face a hostile work environment (bullying, sexual harassment and the like). And work friendships provide a buffer and support for needed whistleblowing.

Researchers at Tel Aviv University followed multiple workers for over two decades, and found that work friendships or lack thereof had more direct influence on our health than any other construct they tracked. As the research participants got older, those with little or no work friends were 2.4 times more likely to die during the study. So while the system sucks, having work friends operates as some needed insulation foam to support the cracks in the system while we do our best to get by. I have a group of friends who I still adore from a crazy-ass workplace. We got each other through and helped get each other out. And every year (many years later!) we have a big Friendsgiving party where we hang out and stuff our faces and cheer our escape success and still enjoy each other's company.

I'm not saying you have to have a nice cuddle with your cubicle mate, but finding the people who are supportive and who you enjoy isn't the worst thing in the world. There are definitely traps to avoid . . . like snarky office gossip, and mean-girling (or mean-boying or mean-enbying) people out of group work projects, and there's a level of overshare you can't take back.

And you definitely don't have to devote non-office hours to these friends unless you genuinely want to. If Happy Hour isn't your thing, thank people for the kind invitation and pass. Doesn't have to be a big deal, maybe "If I don't go to the gym right after work, I won't go at all and that's my therapy" or a lighthearted but vague E. B. White response (who famously said *"I must decline, for secret reasons"* when asked to sit on President

Eisenhower's Arts and Sciences committee) is a perfectly kind boundary statement.

Tia Faith

Dear Auntie Faith,

How do you make friends without alcohol?

Hey friend-person,

Booze as a social lubricant has been exceptionally good for capitalism. And it has especially influenced queer culture. Have you ever heard of Project SCUM? It's a real thing. Go google it real quick, I'll wait here.

SCUM stands for *sub-cultural urban marketing*. Cigarettes and alcohol were marketed specifically in the gayborhoods of the '90s, starting in the Castro and Tenderloin districts of San Francisco. Clubs and bars had been historically safer places for queer folks to congregate and make friends, and capitalism in turn started to reinforce that in specific ways. Now the commercialization of pride month is everywhere, but up until recently it was only booze and tobacco that was marketed thusly. Reinforcing that's where you find queer family.

But drinking is an event in and of itself for all people, especially in the US. The US has historically always had a drinking problem according to a 2021 article in the Atlantic. And being the sober person around a bunch of lit people is not fun, especially if you are newly in recovery yourself.

There has been a movement as of late of sober spaces. And I don't mean the stuff that my middle-aged ass likes to do, like go to bookstores and parks and taco trucks with picnic tables out front. But like non-alcoholic bars that have snacks and fun booze-free cocktails. Of fun #queerandsober and #dragandsober events and concerts. So there are more and more places, in larger cities, where you can go out after dark and have fun without someone spilling their marg all over you. This isn't just a place you can meet up with friends to hang, but also a great way to meet new people. Whether or not they drink, they're comfortable in sober spaces therefore are far more likely to be comfortable with you and your sobriety goals.

If that's not available in your area, and all your people are doing the strip crawl on a friday night, or you are just wanting to dance your ass off but SOBER, there are multiple ways of handling your sobriety without "getting into it." You can say you're doing a Whole30 cleanse so aren't drinking rn. You can carry around a club soda with lime and people will think you're having a gin & tonic and not question why you aren't getting shit-faced with the rest of the group. If you are sober for REASONS, and can maintain that around people that are using without relapse, go for it.

And can I also say? Be the sober friend for other non-drinkers at events. My husband and I don't drink, and if I know someone else is also sober and is going to be at the same event, I'll remind them they can come hang with us at the table where there is no vodka escaping everyone's pores. A lot of people over the years have told me they went to an event because they knew they could hang with Auntie Faith and Uncle Joe at the soda and nachos table. The running story is that Uncle Joe (also known as Mr. Dr. Faith) is a recovery coach so no booze on the table for Facebook photos. He has no problem taking one for the team.

Auntie Faith (and Uncle Joe)

Dear Auntie Faith,

How do people form friend groups? I have always had one-on-one friendships but when I try to introduce my friends to each other there's no chemistry. I long to be part of a group like in the TV show Friends where we all have each others' back.

Hey friend-person,

It's getting harder and harder to create friendship circles like that, isn't it? We're so fast-paced and fucking busy (legitmately!) that one person at a time feels far more manageable. So taking the lead and being the cruise director hasn't worked yet (good for you for putting that out there, though!) and it makes me wonder if the people you tried to introduce to each other genuinely didn't have anything in common or didn't realize that they did. Bringing people together works better when there is a group task or project planned. So it isn't everyone sitting around saying "great wine!" and "yeah great!" back and forth until the end of time.

Something like "I bought a new table top game so I was hoping y'all would help me break the seal on it! Y'all don't know each other but you are all my fellow gamer dorks so I think it would be a fun crowd!" If you think an in person event is "too much" as a start you can try what my teen clients often do, which is start a group chat or, Discord channel, etc., add the people you want to meet to it, and make the intro. As in "Hey, Alex, Taylor, and Tato! Y'all don't know each other yet, but you are all my favorite local foodies and I thought of all of you when I drove by the new ceviche place downtown. Has anyone been yet? Anything else good you discovered recently?" Still a task oriented convo starter but without the in-person pressure.

Also? Your disparate buddies may just remain too disparate to hang with each other. Maybe you're a weirdo who has a diverse collection of weirdos, but they're too diverse to like each other. If that's the case, it might also be helpful to start joining already existent groups like a local hiking group, book club, or whatever you are into (or at least curious about). Not to replace the friends you have, of course, but a local meet-up will introduce you to several people, a few of whom you may really like and can invite out for coffee at Central Perk or to sing Smelly Cat?

Auntie Faith

Dear Auntie Faith,

We know that as humans we are prone to wanting to be accepted by our group, our people. How do we create friendships that don't just lead to more groupthink situations? Does that even make sense?

Hey friend-person,

I hear you saying that as much as having a wonderful group of friends, just like on *Friends*, is total goals you want to make sure that it isn't a group of people who all think and act the same way. The show itself, bless it's head, was full of white, conventionally attractive, straight sized, cisgender, heterosexual men and women in a specific age group.

And we do have a habit of hanging out with people like us. There is a sense of safety and comfort in it. And probably some evolutionary advantage. Some researchers did DNA tests of non-related friends (meaning not like you and your actual biological cousin who is also your best friend), and it turns out that there is evidence that our friends are quite likely to share the same amount of genes with us as a known fourth cousin. Apparently, we sniff out family at some level.

(Did that research freak you out? It freaked me out.)

Challenging that means leaning into discomfort. Going places you don't usually go, striking up conversations with people you wouldn't chat with otherwise, doing shit you wouldn't normally do. And when you meet people unlike you, doing the deep listening required to connect with (and honor!) different life experiences. I answered a letter in this chapter about dealing with trash rhetoric like racism, but let me reiterate I don't mean "they're older so it's okay that they think a nonbinary identity is a sign of mental illness" is something you are required to take on with friends. But different experiences in general lead to richer friend groups, and then larger society. But it starts with looking past the people you notice first.

And thank you for being a friend (I had to make a Golden Girls joke at least once in this book),

Auntie Faith

Citations

Adams, R.G., & Blieszner, R. 1994. An Integrative Conceptual Framework for Friendship

Research. Journal of Social and Personal Relationships, v.11 no.2: 163-184.

Bacon, L. (2020). Radical Belonging. BenBella Books.

Baska, M., Davies, M., Maurice, E. P., Parsons, V., Yates, J., Wakefield, L., & Mitchell, H. (2019, June 26). How to tell if you're in a quasiplatonic relationship. PinkNews. https://www.pinknews.co.uk/2018/04/18/what-is-a-quasiplatonic-aka-queerplatonic-relationship-friendship/.

Blieszner, R., Ogletree, A. M., & Adams, R. G. (2019). Friendship in Later Life: A Research Agenda. Innovation in aging, 3(1), igz005. https://doi.org/10.1093/geroni/igz005

Boudreau, D. (2011, May 23). Deconstructing friendship. Retrieved April 08, 2021, from https://research.asu.edu/deconstructing-friendship

Brake, E. (2012). Minimizing marriage, morality, and the law. Oxford: Oxford University Press.

Brown, William & Bocarnea, Mihai. (2006). Celebrity-Persona Parasocial Interaction Scale. 10.4018/978-1-59140-792-8.ch039.

Carlson, J., & Dermer, S. B. (2017). In The SAGE encyclopedia of marriage, family, and couples counseling. essay, SAGE Publications, Inc.

Cornwall, G. (2020, November 18). What the research says about the academic power of friendship - mindshift. Retrieved April 07, 2021, from https://www.kqed.org/mindshift/56979/what-the-research-says-about-the-academic-power-of-friendship

Degges-White, S. (2018, May 29). Friendology: The science of friendship. Retrieved April 07, 2021, from https://www.psychologytoday.com/us/blog/lifetime-connections/201805/friendology-the-science-friendship

Derrick, J. L., Gabriel, S., & Hugenberg, K. (2009). Social surrogacy: How favored television programs provide the experience of belonging. Journal of Experimental Social Psychology, 45(2), 352-362. doi:10.1016/j.jesp.2008.12.003

Dunbar, R. I. M. (1992). "Neocortex size as a constraint on group size in primates". Journal of Human Evolution. 22 (6): 469–493. doi:10.1016/0047-2484(92)90081-J.

Friendships pose unique challenges for women on the spectrum. Spectrum. (2019, August 28). https://www.spectrumnews.org/opinion/viewpoint/friendships-pose-unique-challenges-women-spectrum/.

Khazan, O. (2017, April 07). How loneliness makes you worse at social interaction. Retrieved April 07, 2021, from https://www.theatlantic.com/health/archive/2017/04/how-loneliness-begets-loneliness/521841/

Hall, J. A. (2019). How many hours does it take to make a friend? Journal of Social and Personal Relationships, 36(4), 1278–1296. https://doi.org/10.1177/0265407518761225

Hall, J. A., & Davis, D. A. C. (in press). Proposing the Communicate Bond Belong Theory: Evolutionary intersections with episodic interpersonal communication. Communication Theory. doi:10.1111/comt.12106

Hartmann, Tilo; Goldhoorn, Charlotte (December 2011). "Horton and Wohl Revisited: Exploring Viewers' Experience of Parasocial Interaction". Journal of Communication. 61 (6): 1104–1121. doi:10.1111/j.1460-2466.2011.01595.x.

Hawkley, L. C., & Cacioppo, J. T. (2010). Loneliness matters: a theoretical and empirical review of consequences and mechanisms. Annals of behavioral medicine: a publication of the Society of Behavioral Medicine, 40(2), 218–227. https://doi.org/10.1007/s12160-010-9210-8

Heintzelman, S. J., & King, L. A. (2014). Life is pretty meaningful. American Psychologist, 69(6), 561–574. https://doi.org/10.1037/a0035049

How loneliness can make you sick. (n.d.). Retrieved April 15, 2021, from https://www.apa.org/science/about/psa/2017/09/loneliness-sicko

Hruschka, D. J. (2010). Friendship: Development, Ecology, and Evolution of a Relationship (Origins of human behavior and culture ; 5). University of California Press.

Julian, K. (2021, June 4). America Has a Drinking Problem. The Atlantic. https://www.theatlantic.com/magazine/archive/2021/07/america-drinking-alone-problem/619017/

Khalil, R., Tindle, R., Boraud, T., Moustafa, A. A., & Karim, A. A. (2018). Social decision making in autism: On the impact of mirror neurons, motor control, and imitative behaviors. CNS

Neuroscience & Therapeutics, 24(8), 669–676. https://doi. org/10.1111/cns.13001

Kreager, D., Molloy, L., Moody, J., & Feinberg, M. (2015). Friends First? The Peer Network Origins of Adolescent Dating. Journal of Research on Adolescence, 26(2), 257–269. https://doi.org/10.1111/jora.12189

Kilner, J. M., & Lemon, R. N. (2013). What we know currently about mirror neurons. Current biology : CB, 23(23), R1057–R1062. https://doi.org/10.1016/j.cub.2013.10.051

Levine, A. (2019). Attached. Bluebird.

Liebers, N.; Schramm, H. (2019). "Parasocial Interactions and Relationships with Media Characters-An Inventory of 60 Years of Research". Communication Research Trends. 38 (2): 4–31.

Liu, W. T., & Duff, R. W. (1972). The strength in weak ties. Public Opinion Quarterly, 36(3), 361. doi:10.1086/268018

Menakem, R. (2021). My grandmother's hands: Racialized trauma and the pathway to mending our hearts and bodies. London: Penguin Books.

Miller, J. B. (1991). Toward a new psychology of women. Penguin Books.

Miritello, G., Lara, R., Cebrian, M. et al. Limited communication capacity unveils strategies for human interaction. Sci Rep 3, 1950 (2013). https://doi.org/10.1038/srep01950

Morin, A. (2017, August 7). 7 Science-Backed Reasons You Should Spend More Time Alone. Forbes. https://www.forbes.com/sites/amymorin/2017/08/05/7-science-backed-reasons-you-should-spend-more-time-alone/?sh=641132071b7e.

Mull, A. (2021, January 29). The pandemic has erased entire categories of friendship. Retrieved April 06, 2021, from https://www.theatlantic.com/health/archive/2021/01/pandemic-goodbye-casual-friends/617839/

My Thoughts on the Word "Zucchini". Writing From Factor X. (2011, July 12). https://writingfromfactorx.wordpress.com/2011/07/11/my-thoughts-on-the-word-zucchini/.

National Academies of Sciences, Engineering, and Medicine. 2020. Social Isolation and Loneliness in Older Adults: Opportunities for the Health Care System. Washington, DC: The National Academies Press. https://doi.org/10.17226/25663external icon.

Nietlisbach, G., & Maercker, A. (2009). Social Cognition and Interpersonal Impairments in Trauma Survivors with PTSD.

Journal of Aggression, Maltreatment & Trauma, 18(4), 382–402. https://doi.org/10.1080/10926770902881489

Ortiz-Ospina, E., & Roser, M. (2020, February 14). Loneliness and social connections. Retrieved April 15, 2021, from https://ourworldindata.org/social-connections-and-loneliness

Patook blog - how hard is it to make friends. (n.d.). Retrieved April 15, 2021, from https://patook.com/Blog/MakingFriends

Pattee, E. (2019, November 20). How to have closer friendships (and why you need them). Retrieved April 07, 2021, from https://www.nytimes.com/2019/11/20/smarter-living/how-to-have-closer-friendships.html

Petersen, A. (2020, February 09). The Surprising Science Behind Friendship. Retrieved April 06, 2021, from https://www.wsj.com/articles/the-surprising-science-behind-friendship-11581256802

Programs. Go to Parenting Success Network. (n.d.). https://www.parentingsuccessnetwork.org/the-power-of-attunement/.

Queerplatonic Relationship. Aromantics Wiki. (n.d.). https://aromantic.wikia.org/wiki/Queerplatonic_Relationship#cite_note-1.

Rana, Z. (n.d.). Aristotle said there are three types of friendship, but only one we should strive for. Retrieved April 07, 2021, from https://qz.com/1155649/aristotle-said-there-are-three-types-of-friendship-but-only-one-we-should-strive-for/

Rosqvist, H. B., Brownlow, C., & O´Dell, L. (n.d.). "What's the point of having friends?": Reformulating Notions of the Meaning of Friends and Friendship among Autistic People. Disability Studies Quarterly. https://dsq-sds.org/article/view/3254/4109.

Seppälä, E. & King, M. K. M. (n.d.). Are Work Friendships a Good Thing? Greater Good. https://greatergood.berkeley.edu/article/item/are_work_friendships_a_good_thing.

Schawbel, D. (2018, November 13). Why work friendships are critical for long-term happiness . CNBC. https://www.cnbc.com/2018/11/13/why-work-friendships-are-critical-for-long-term-happiness.html.

Smith, S. (2016, March 25). I Don't Mean to Baffle You, But I Do: Queerplatonic Partnerships. this ain't livin'. http://meloukhia.net/2012/06/i_dont_mean_to_baffle_you_but_i_do_queerplatonic_partnerships/.

Solving the Hidden disease that's as bad as 15 cigarettes a day. (2019, November 26). Retrieved April 15, 2021, from https://

www.ozy.com/news-and-politics/solving-the-hidden-disease-thats-as-bad-as-15-cigarettes-a-day/88903/.

Sussex Publishers. (n.d.). Finding Connection Through "Chosen Family". Psychology Today. https://www.psychologytoday.com/us/blog/being-unlonely/201906/finding-connection-through-chosen-family.

Sussex Publishers. (n.d.). Easing Your Way Out of Loneliness. Psychology Today. https://www.psychologytoday.com/us/blog/connections/200812/easing-your-way-out-loneliness.

TheRSA. (n.d.). Look into my eyes: what attunement means for communication. The RSA. https://www.thersa.org/blog/2013/01/look-in-to-my-eyes-what-attunement-means-for-communication.

More by Dr. Faith

Books
The Autism Relationships Handbook (with Joe Biel)
Coping Skills
How to Be Accountable (with Joe Biel)
This Is Your Brain on Depression
Unfuck Your Adulting
Unfuck Your Anger
Unfuck Your Anxiety
Unfuck Your Blow Jobs
Unfuck Your Body
Unfuck Your Boundaries
Unfuck Your Brain
Unfuck Your Cunnilingus
Unfuck Your Grief
Unfuck Your Friendships
Unfuck Your Intimacy
Unfuck Your Worth
Unfuck Your Writing (with Joe Biel)
Woke Parenting (with Bonnie Scott)

Workbooks
Achieve Your Goals
The Autism Relationships Workbook (with Joe Biel)
How to Be Accountable Workbook (with Joe Biel)
Unfuck Your Anger Workbook
Unfuck Your Anxiety Workbook
Unfuck Your Body Workbook
Unfuck Your Boundaries Workbook
Unfuck Your Intimacy Workbook
Unfuck Your Worth Workbook
Unfuck Your Year

Other
Boundaries Conversation Deck
How Do You Feel Today? (poster)

Zines
The Autism Handbook (with Joe Biel)
The Autism Partner Handbook (with Joe Biel)
BDSM FAQ
Dating
Defriending
Detox Your Masculinity (with Aaron Sapp)
Emotional Freedom Technique
The Five Emotional Hungers
Getting Over It
How to Find a Therapist
How to Say No
Indigenous Noms
Relationshipping
The Revolution Won't Forget the Holidays
Self-Compassion
Sex Tools
Sexing Yourself
STI FAQ (with Aaron Sapp)
Surviving
This Is Your Brain on Addiction
This Is Your Brain on Grief
This Is Your Brain on PTSD
Unfuck Your Consent
Unfuck Your Forgiveness
Unfuck Your Mental Health Paradigm
Unfuck Your Sleep
Unfuck Your Stress
Unfuck Your Work
Vision Boarding
Woke Parenting #1-6 (with Bonnie Scott)

ABOUT THE AUTHOR

Faith Harper PhD, LPC-S, ACS, ACN is a bad-ass, funny lady with a PhD. She's a licensed professional counselor, board supervisor, certified sexologist, and applied clinical nutritionist with a private practice and consulting business in San Antonio, TX. She has been an adjunct professor and a TEDx presenter, and proudly identifies as a woman of color and uppity intersectional feminist. She is the author of dozens of books.

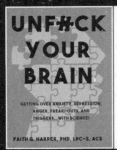

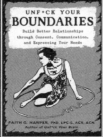
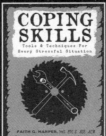